HEBDEN E
PICTURE 1_ _ _ _ _ _

THE LIFE & TIMES
OF
A LOCAL TREASURE

Image of the Picture House by Dave Woodsworth-Dale

This is a Friends of the Picture House Publication

Website: www.hebdenbridgepicturehouse.co.uk/friends
Email: foph@hebdenbridgepicturehouse.co.uk
Facebook: www.facebook.com/FriendsOfThePictureHouse
Twitter: @FriendsofPH

Hebden Bridge Picture House, 2016, photograph taken by Raphael Pavel, http://www.raphaeloo.com/

HEBDEN BRIDGE PICTURE HOUSE

THE LIFE AND TIMES
OF
A LOCAL TREASURE

Kate Higham & Ray Barnes

Published in the United Kingdom by:
The Friends of the Picture House

First Edition November, 2016

Printed by Axis
Brighouse
HD6 2SD

ISBN 978-1-5272-0299-3

CONTENTS

Acknowledgements

We would like to thank all of the many people who have helped to make this book possible.

Rebekah Fozard, Manager of the Picture House, Graham Tottles, projectionist, and all of the staff at the cinema. Thank-you for your help, for your openness in sharing memories, and for your warmth and enthusiasm for the project

Diana Monahan, Hebden Bridge Local History Society, for sharing her expertise with us, and for her generous help with this venture.

Everyone who has allowed us to interview them and shared their memories with us, and all those who have allowed their photographs to be used to illustrate and inform the text

Pennine Heritage, Frank Woolrych

Martin Parr for generously allowing us to use his photographs

Bruce Cutts and the After Alice Project

Maurice Robson, former Manager of the Picture House

Ross Mackintosh for cover design

Martin Allan at Axis Printing for help and advice

Raphael Pavel, Dave Woodsworth-Dale

Sarah Mason Photography

Jason Boom, Town Clerk, Hebden Royd Town Council

The Friends of the Picture House Committee (2016) - Paul Knights, Fyfe Sainsbury, Jill Osman, Maggie Woods, Moya O'Donnell, Mike Troke, Rachel O'Hare, Donna Sidonio, Daniel & Nicola Law, Emily Watnick, Allen Keep, Sue Carter, Ashleigh Cooper

Chris Ratcliffe, photographs from HebWeb

Daniel Birch

All those knowledgeable folk on the 'Old Photos of Halifax' Facebook page and 'HistoryPin' who helped us to track down details of long-forgotten cinemas

Cinema Treasures and Malcom Bull's Calderdale Companion

Johnny Meynell, Steve Gee

West Yorkshire Calderdale Archives

Jez Lewis, Michael Silcock,

Clive Polden, Paul Haywood

Roland Higham for technical assistance

Sheila Higham for proof-reading

Lorna Higham and Aimee Higham, photographic assistants

Foreword

Since joining the committee of the voluntary group the Friends of the Picture House in 2011, and chairing it for the past two years, it has been my hope that we could put together a history of our town's glorious cinema. As it approaches its centenary, this icon of our community deserves to have its story told. I had in mind a leaflet, or at most a small booklet. But even this seemed a tall order, since local history research, properly done, is a painstaking and time-consuming business, and the Friends group was always absorbed in other projects to support the cinema. I was so glad when Kate, a central member of the Friends committee since 2013, and her father, Ray, took on this project. Soon after they began their research it became clear that their incredible dedication to telling the tale accurately and to doing justice to the people we have to thank for the cinema surviving through the difficult times, was going to gift us not with a leaflet or a booklet but the wonderful book you hold in your hands. Thanks to Kate and Ray, the Picture House and its champions now have their story told in the way they deserve.

As well as tracing the Picture House's story against the background of a century of Hebden Bridge history, Kate and Ray also place it within the context of the development of the British cinema industry. What becomes clear as you read is that the early part of the Picture House's story is very representative of the development of UK cinema. It was built at a boom time for the industry, and enjoyed forty years of large audiences. But come the mid-1960s, as social and technological change posed serious challenges to the cinema industry, its story becomes more exceptional simply because it survived. There have been over 6,000 cinemas in the UK. If we discount the modern multiplexes owned by the big chains, the Picture House is one of only 400 of its kind remaining. Our local area was not immune to these huge losses; Kate and Ray's research found over 30 cinemas within 10 miles of Hebden Bridge, only two of which are now open and operating principally as a cinema. This book, therefore, tells a tale of survival against enormous odds.

What it does so well is make clear that this survival was not by chance, but a combination of the passion and loyalty of local people, far-sighted and public-minded local councillors, and the careful stewarding of a succession of excellent managers and cinema staff. For our part, the Friends group is the latest incarnation of the campaigning spirit of local people without which the Picture House would certainly have closed, just like thousands of others, some time in the last 50 years. Thankfully, given Hebden Royd Town Council's wholehearted support for the cinema, our activities can be directed towards improving rather than defending it. Through a Christmas raffle (which Kate masterminds every year), and other fundraising activities and donations, we have raised £13,000 for improvements at the cinema, detailed in these pages. These funds have come almost entirely from cinema-goers who give generously because they love the Picture House. In this book you will read of that same love and loyalty that has been needed over the years to save it from the threat of closure time and time again.

This book is published just as the Picture House is emerging from the formidable challenge of recovering from the devastation wreaked on it by the Boxing Day floods of 2015. This could easily have been the end, but through the incredible work of the management, the staff and scores of volunteers who helped in the immediate aftermath, and with the support of the Town Council, it now looks better than ever and is ready for the future.

But now the trailers are over and the feature is about to start. In true Picture House fashion before you settle down to read, get yourself a mug of tea and a cake. You are in for a treat: a Kate Higham and Ray Barnes production, with a cast of thousands, starring the inimitable Hebden Bridge Picture House in a generations-spanning epic tale of passion, loyalty and survival....I can see the movie now.

Paul Knights
Chair of the Friends of the Picture House

Above, David Atherton, Duty Manager at the Picture House, 2016, photograph courtesy of Bruce Cutts, After Alice Project

Anne Evans and David Atherton at work in the Picture House, 2016, photograph courtesy of Bruce Cutts, After Alice Project

Introduction

Some of the most popular avenues of entertainment in Edwardian Britain included music hall, concerts and drama. Attending such events could be expensive, however, and so the arrival of 'moving pictures' provided a much cheaper alternative. Cinemas were springing up all over the country in the early part of the twentieth century. Some, like the Hippodrome theatre in Todmorden, began by screening film interludes as part of the drama programme. Such short films were first shown at the Hippodrome in 1911 and by 1917 film shows had taken over as the main entertainment.

When sound arrived, the Hippodrome was the first cinema in Todmorden to present 'talkies' with 'Broadway Melody' on 17th March 1930.

Across the country, around the 1920's and 30's, we see the construction of many purpose-built cinemas designed to resemble monumental palaces with marble walls, ornate interior decoration and imposing entrances. There was, quite often, accommodation for over 1,000 people seated in comfort. The largest of these single screen cinemas was Green's Playhouse in Glasgow, which opened in 1927 with 4,254 seats!

These picture palaces, with their plush carpets and seating, ornate decor - warm in winter and cool in summer - must have been the epitome of luxury to people living in houses with no central heating or bathroom and the toilet outside in the yard!

The public flocked to the cinema during the 1930's, 40's and early 50's. It provided entertainment, access to news and a view into the lives of celebrities, politicians and the Royal Family.

With the increasing popularity of television in the mid to late 1950's and later the availability of films on home video, cinema's popularity waned and attendances plummeted. In 1950 the number of cinemas in Britain was nearly 5,000. By

1960, the number had decreased to 3,000 and by 1965 it had fallen to 2,000. By 2014 there were just 740 cinemas operating in Britain.

In 1985, the U.K.'s first purpose-built 'multiplex' cinema opened. The Point at Milton Keynes boasted ten screens and included restaurants, a bar and a night club. It operated for 30 years but was closed when the nearby IMAX cinema opened.

The steep decline in cinema attendances is evident from this graph. Since 2003, however, the level has remained remarkably steady at just under 200 million attendances per year.

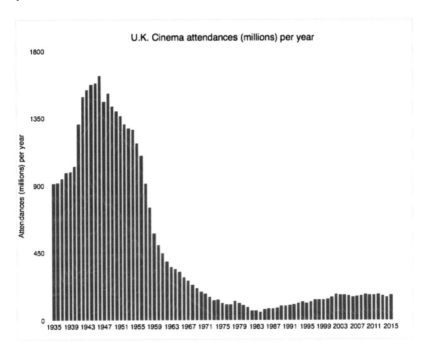

Data from U.K. Cinema Association 'Industry Facts & Figures', 2015 (1)

The problem for cinema owners is how to tap into this fund of filmgoers. The multiplex cinemas endeavour to obtain films immediately after release while public interest is at its highest. They also use add-on attractions such as easy parking, restaurants, bars and nightclubs.

The single screen independent cinemas have a more difficult job. Their management teams need to connect with the local community, to cater for diverse groups of people, to stage special events and to build up a loyal following in order to have a chance of staying afloat. They can also offer friendly service, comfort and the kind of old time atmosphere that multiplexes cannot provide.

It is against this backdrop that the story of our Picture House is set. After starting life in 1921 it has defied 'the slings and arrows of outrageous fortune', and survived where many other similar establishments have failed.

Although this is the story of this one particular cinema, its life does, in fact, mirror that of the industry as a whole. It has endured from its beginnings early in the 20th century, through its halcyon years in the 1940's and early 50's, through the difficult times of the latter part of the century and into the changes that were forced on the industry in the 21st century.

So take your seats, sit back, read on, and discover the story behind Hebden Bridge Picture House.

1. Silent Dawn

"A strange thing has happened - while all the other arts were born naked, this, the youngest, has been born fully-clothed. It can say everything before it has anything to say. It is as if the savage tribe, instead of finding two bars of iron to play with, had found scattering the seashore fiddles, flutes, saxophones, trumpets, grand pianos by Erard and Bechstein, and had begun with incredible energy, but without knowing a note of music, to hammer and thump upon them all at the same time."
Virginia Woolf, 1926 (2)

These were some of Virginia Woolf's thoughts on cinema, when it was still young and silent - an emerging art-form, the so-called 'seventh art'.

If we are to properly tell the story of our Picture House in Hebden Bridge, we must begin here, with the birth of cinema itself, back in those days when it was new and amazing - exciting, but slightly unnerving for people not used to such technology.

Leeds has been identified by many as the birthplace of cinematography. In 1888, the French inventor, Louis Le Prince, whilst working at his wife's family's engineering firm, succeeded in producing moving picture images. Using a camera that he had designed himself, he filmed the Whitley family in the garden of their home in Oakwood Grange Road, Roundhay. He later also shot a sequence showing traffic crossing Leeds Bridge. This was before the work of Louis Lumière and Thomas Edison.

Le Prince was never able to take the credit for his invention because he and all of his equipment mysteriously disappeared while on a train journey in France. His body was never found and murder was suspected, but never proved. These historic films can be now be seen at the Armley Mills Industrial Museum, Leeds. Le Prince was the subject of a

2015 film, 'The First Film', which claims him as the real inventor of the moving image, and is interesting viewing.

1.1 Six frame sequence of Leeds Bridge, 1888, by Louis Le Prince, National Media Museum/Science & Society Picture Library

The Lumière brothers are credited by some as being the first true *film-makers* in history. Their 'Cinématographe' was patented in 1895. They put on a paid showing of their films in Paris and then went on tour with the Cinématographe in 1896, visiting Brussels, Bombay, London, Montreal, New York and Buenos Aires. At the Regent Cinema in London, fifty-four people each paid a shilling to watch silent, grainy, unsteady forty second long scenes of ordinary life, filmed by the Lumière Brothers. These films were cranked through a projector by hand.

1.2 Auguste and Louis Lumière, Public Domain

11

In the years that followed the public embraced this cutting-edge technology and demand grew for this new brand of entertainment. Some of the first early experiments in showing these new 'moving pictures' for entertainment were, in fact, carried out in the music halls of late Victorian England. Short films were increasingly included in the programme alongside the live music hall acts. Production companies would sell their films outright to music hall exhibitors for a shilling a foot, regardless of subject!

One of the foremost film-making entrepreneurs in the UK at this time was Robert Paul, a London instrument maker, who pioneered a system of projecting motion pictures onto a screen. Paul constructed Britain's first film studios in Muswell Hill, North London and produced many short dramatic films there. One of his 1896 films featured cartoonist, Tom Merry, drawing caricatures of the German Emperor, Kaiser Wilhelm II, and Prince Bismarck. Merry had previously performed his lightning-fast drawing as part of a music hall stage act. Paul's 'Theatrograph' system, the first commercially produced 35mm projector, became very popular in music halls throughout the country.

1.3 (left) Paul's Theatrograph, National Media Museum/ Science & Society Picture Library

1.4 (right) Music Hall poster, National Media Museum/ Science & Society Picture Library

The residents of Hebden Bridge were first given the chance to watch moving pictures around 1900 when a travelling theatre, 'Blake's Alhambra', arrived in town. It is likely that, in addition to the programme of live dramatics, short films were screened there using Paul's Theatrograph.

So what would these travelling performers have found as their wagons rolled into Hebden Bridge at the turn of the last century? What type of place was it and what were its origins?

The first settlements in the area were actually on the hilltops as the bottom of the valley was waterlogged and swampy. There was very little building on the valley floor until 1314, when a mill was constructed next to the bridge across the river Hebden. The site of this mill is where 'Innovation' shop and café now stand. This site was important as it was the point where the main packhorse track from Halifax to Burnley crossed the river. These tracks would have been used by farmers from the hillsides bringing their crops of oats to be ground in the mill and also by packhorse trains carrying wool or cloth.

© PHDA - Steven Brook Collection

1.5 Bridge Mill, Hebden Bridge, c.1980, Steven Brook Collection

In 1510, the original wooden bridge had been so heavily used as to be unsafe, so funds were raised to build the stone bridge we see in the centre of town today.

1.6 Old Bridge, Hebden Bridge c.1870, Alice Longstaff Gallery Collection

Such was the situation until the seventeenth century when drainage techniques became more advanced and farming could begin on the valley floor. In 1657, Kings Farm was built next to the mill. This soon also began to function as an inn for the increasing numbers of passing travellers. This inn still survives today as the White Lion.

1.7 White Lion Hotel, Hebden Bridge, c.1900, Alice Longstaff Gallery Collection

Turnpikes were set up to replace the old packhorse tracks. Then canal and railway links were established in 1795 and 1841, respectively. These developments ensured good communication and transport channels. The town grew rapidly, establishing itself as a centre for the textile industry, especially for the production of fustian cloth. Hebden Bridge became nicknamed 'Fustianopolis' or 'Trouser-Town'. Business boomed and the town continued to grow through the rest of the nineteenth century. The travelling performers of Blake's Alhambra would have arrived in a small, thriving market town, well-connected by road, rail and waterway, already one of the principal components of the textile industry in the country.

These travelling theatre companies would have provided the first taste of cinematic entertainment for Hebden Bridge. As cinemas began to open in the rest of the country and film-making techniques became more sophisticated, it is not surprising that the townspeople soon wanted a picture house of their own.

As film at that time was nitrate-based and thus highly flammable, fire was a not infrequent hazard when films became hot in the projector. The Cinematograph Act of 1910 stated that where the public were paying to watch films, a fire-resistant projection booth must be in place. Following the introduction of this act, a licence was required to open a cinema and many purpose-built cinemas began to spring up. Indeed, on the 30th August 1911, Hebden Bridge Urban District Council approved the erection of a picture house in Thistle Holme Field, on New Road, opposite the tram terminus. There must have been some reservations regarding this form of entertainment at the time, as approval was given for this to operate for only three years from the date of its completion. The plans submitted for the construction state, 'Temporary Picture Hall'.

1.8 View of Hebden Bridge c.1880 showing Thistle Holme Field pre-development, Alice Longstaff Collection

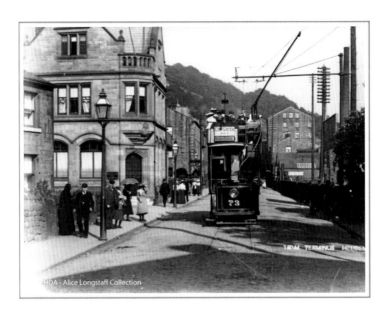

1.9 Tram terminus on New Road, Hebden Bridge, c.1910, Alice Longstaff Collection

1.10 The Royal Electric Theatre and Hippodrome, 1913, Alice Longstaff Collection

The result was a timber building with quite an imposing front. It was designed by local architect, W.H. Cockcroft, and built by Messrs. Wadsworth and Shaw. It was given the grand title, 'The Royal Electric Theatre and Hippodrome', but was more often referred to locally as the 'Wood Hut'. It opened its doors on 17th December 1912, screening, of course, silent films while a pianist played accompaniment.

As we can see from these views (below) of the original plans for the Royal Electric Theatre, the entrance was at the front of the building with a small pay booth. At the rear of the auditorium there was a section of tiered seating with a flat area in front of the screen. Particular note is made of the fire-proof projection booth to comply with the legal requirements of such a building. The ladies toilet is indoors, whilst the gentlemen's convenience is situated outside, perhaps indicating chivalry on the part of Mr Cockcroft!

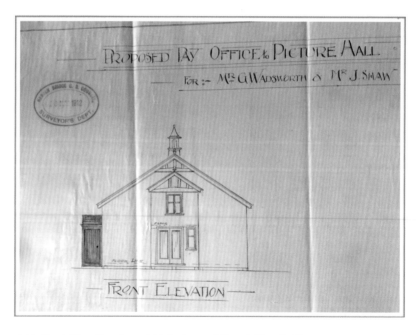

1.11 Front Elevation from initial plans of Royal Electric Theatre, West Yorkshire Archive Service, Calderdale

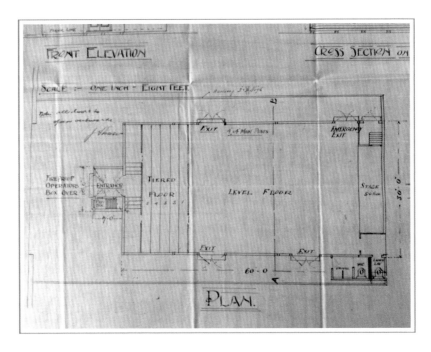

1.12 Floor plan of Royal Electric Theatre, West Yorkshire Archive Service, Calderdale

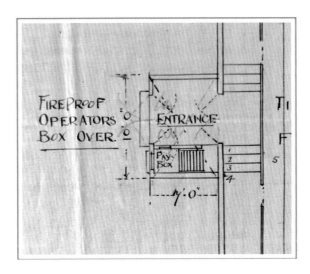

1.13 Plans showing fireproof projection room, West Yorkshire Archive Service, Calderdale

Presumably, as cinema gained in popularity, the plans for the building became increasingly ambitious. The initial plans, dated August 1911, show a small building with a simple facade (see 1.11). However, during the building process further plans were submitted (in September 1912) for a larger construction with a much more elaborate frontage (see below).

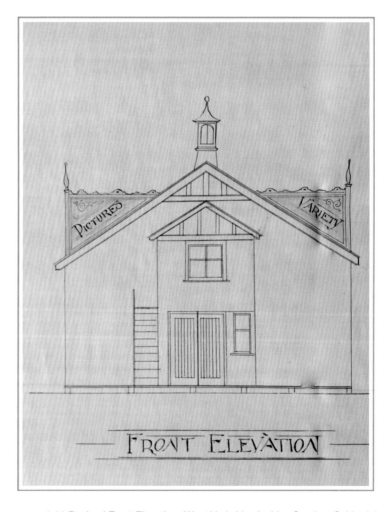

1.14 Revised Front Elevation, West Yorkshire Archive Service, Calderdale

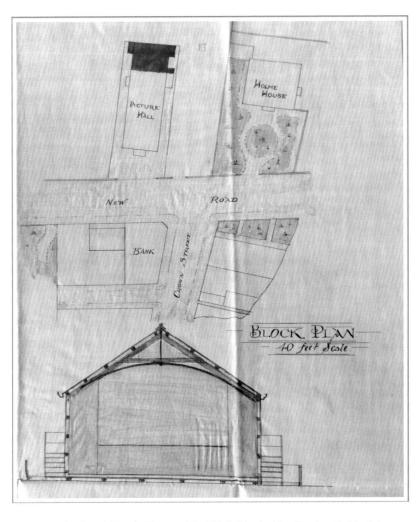

1.15 Plan for Royal Electric Theatre, West Yorkshire Archive Service, Calderdale

21

There are a number of recorded memories of the early days of cinema at the Royal Electric. One Wilfred Manning, a local film-goer, wrote:

"It was a wooden building painted red, known as 'T'Blood Tup'. Near by the old 'Royal Electric' used to be the U.C.P. tripe shop where we could get a 'pennorth' of tripe bits. Also for a penny we could go to the fish and chip shop for a 'penny slosh' which was a saucer of chips covered in black peas and gravy."

Fred Crossley, another regular film-goer wrote:

"In 1913, the chief source of entertainment was the local 'Royal Electric Cinema'. This was a large timber building with a palatial front situated in fields close to the tram terminus. They were, of course, silent films. We used to occupy the cheapest front seats which were wooden forms with a back rest. Before the performance was over the seats became very hard and some people took a cushion to sit on. The accompaniment to the pictures was a piano being played. The price of admission to the front seats was threepence in the evenings and one penny on Saturday afternoon matinee.

Occasionally we used to 'dodge in' when the attendant had temporarily left the pay box. I remember some of the titles of the thrilling pictures. There was 'Phantoms', 'Zigamah', and episodes each week of 'Exploits of Elaine' and 'The Clutching Hand'. Each evening one of the attendants would call out to the audience, "The quarter-to-ten tram is now in!" This was for the benefit of those people who lived two miles away in Mytholmroyd or further afield." (3)

Cinema was also arriving in the rest of the region and, indeed, the country, at this time. In 1914, there were four thousand licensed cinemas in the UK. The day before our own Royal Electric opened its doors, the Central Picture House in Elland also began business. This cinema is still open as the Rex, although it closed and served its time as a bingo hall before being re-opened as a cinema in 1988. In 1911, the Todmorden

Hippodrome began film interludes as part of the live theatre programme, and by 1917, films had taken over as the main entertainment. In Bacup, the Public Hall began screening films in September 1910. It became known as the Gem Cinema but was renamed the Kozy Picture House in 1916.

Very soon the Royal Electric also had more local competition for cinema audiences. The Co-op Hall in Crown Street (now 'Oasis' supermarket) had applied for a stage play licence in 1908. This had been refused, but in January 1913, that is, a few weeks after the opening of the Royal Electric, they were granted permission to show films there.

1.16 Co-op Hall, Crown Street (now 'Oasis' supermarket), c.1960, Hebden Bridge Camera Club

One of the early successes at the Co-op Hall was the heart-rending story of 'Helen of Four Gates' which played to packed audiences. This film was directed by that pioneer of early motion pictures, Cecil Hepworth.

'Helen of Four Gates' was based on a novel by former mill girl, Ethel Carnie Holdsworth. Hepworth used the Pennine moors around Heptonstall and Hebden Bridge for the film's location and local people provided the extras. The film's intertitles (pieces of filmed printed text edited into the photographed action) were printed in the original West Yorkshire dialect that was used in the novel. Actress Alma Taylor starred in the dual role of mother and daughter. This particular film has a tale of its own to tell, but more of that later in our story.

1.17 A Scene from 'Helen of Four Gates', 1920, Copyright Hepworth

2. A Fine Place

"What is saved in the cinema when it achieves art is a spontaneous continuity with all mankind. It is not an art of the princes or the bourgeoisie. It is popular and vagrant. In the sky of the cinema people learn what they might have been and discover what belongs to them apart from their single lives."
John Berger (4)

The First World War was a difficult time for cinemas in the U.K. This may have been due to several factors. There were problems with the supply of new films due to the Atlantic blockade and a general shortage of staff due to conscription. Also, an 'Amusement Tax' was introduced in Britain in 1916 to raise money for the war effort. This meant that entry to entertainment venues was taxed, so tickets for the cinema would have cost more than previously. Despite these obstacles, the Royal Electric Theatre and Hippodrome in Hebden Bridge continued to thrive.

In 1917, cinema was examined by the National Council of Public Morals. The following quote from that report helps us to understand the massive cultural impact that the dawning of cinema had on our society:

"It may be doubted if there is even yet sufficient realisation of the strong and permanent grip which the picture palace has taken upon the people of this country. All other forms of recreation appeal only to a section of the community but the lure of the pictures is universal; while the cheapness and accessibility of the houses make it possible for the masses to indulge in this enjoyment almost to an unlimited extent. In the course of our inquiry we have been much impressed by the evidence brought before us that moving pictures are having a profound influence upon the mental and moral outlook of millions of our young people - no social problem of the day demands more earnest attention."(5)

The conclusion of the report was that films encouraged juvenile crime, the spread of disease and indecent behaviour in the dark! It was, however, thought that the cinema countered the attraction of drinking establishments somewhat, so it couldn't be all bad!

Immediately after the end of the war, there was a ban on the building of 'luxury buildings', including theatres and cinemas. This was imposed in order to encourage the building of much-needed private family housing. Cinema, as an art form and a source of entertainment, continued to gain in popularity however, and as soon as the ban was lifted the construction of ever larger, more ornate, more luxurious cinemas began all over the country. This trend was mirrored in events in Hebden Bridge at this time.

In 1919, the local Thistle Holme Estate Company submitted plans to replace the Royal Electric Theatre with a much grander nine hundred and fifty seat cinema. Once these plans had been accepted by the Town Council the cinema we know today was built on New Road, alongside the old Royal Electric Theatre. The new 'Picture House' was designed by local architects, Messrs. Sutcliffe & Sutcliffe. Local contractors were used for the construction of the cinema. The building work was done by Oldfield Watson, whose builders yard was adjacent to the new cinema. Decoration was by Wrigley & Sons, plumbing by Greenwood & Taylor, and woodwork by Robertshaw Greenwood. The projection equipment was obtained from The Precision Machine Co. of New York, USA

SUTCLIFFE & SUTCLIFFE.
ARCHITECTS.
—
Telephone 38.

NEW ROAD,
HEBDEN BRIDGE.

2.1 Letterhead from architects Sutcliffe & Sutcliffe, Hebden Bridge Local History Society Archive, Architects' Collection Stationery

2.2 Compliment slip from builders, Oldfield Watson, Hebden Bridge Local History
Society Archive, BL6

2.3 Compliment slip from decorators, Wrigley & Sons, Hebden Bridge Local History
Society Archive, Architects' Collection, Q30

2.4 Compliment slip from plumbers, Greenwood & Taylor, Hebden Bridge Local History
Society Archive, Architects' Collection, H86

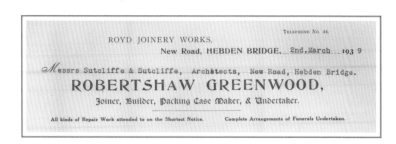

2.5 Compliment slip from joiners, Robertshaw Greenwood, Hebden Bridge Local
History Society Archive, H98

2.6 Oldfield Watson Builders Yard with the Picture House in the background, Hebden
Bridge Camera Club

As the new Picture House opened, the Royal Electric
Theatre and Hippodrome closed and was sold off to become a
billiard hall. The little wooden cinema was eventually
demolished and the site cleared to make way for the
construction of the memorial gardens, which were opened in
August 1938.

2.7 Memorial Gardens opening day, 10th August 1938, Alice Longstaff Collection

The exterior of the new Picture House was Classical in appearance; the front section built of stone with a recessed central section reached by a flight of eleven steps. Giant Doric columns and pilasters supported a heavy entablature which continued on either side to project over side wings with shop accommodation.

Interestingly, when Peter Thornborrow, Senior Historic Buildings Officer, examined the building for an English Heritage listing report in 1999, he noted the details above, but also considered the cinema to be consciously designed to form a harmonious balance with the Hope Baptist Chapel which stands on the opposite side of New Road.

An example of architectural harmony?

2.8 (left) Hebden Bridge Picture House, Kate Higham
2.9 (right) Hope Baptist Church, Hebden Bridge, Kate HIgham

In this era, the USA had already well-established movie studios in Hollywood and countless flamboyant cinemas in its towns and cities. When British architects came to design cinemas they were often based on these American examples already in existence. This may be why the Picture House in Hebden Bridge is a relatively large ornate cinema for what would have been a small market town in the 1920's.

The curved balcony at the rear of the auditorium was constructed with reinforced concrete, this being a very early example of the use of this material in entertainment venues such as this. The strength of steel reinforced concrete allowed the balcony to be constructed on a cantilever basis, without the need for supporting columns. These columns are a problem in theatres and cinemas because they restrict the view of any audience members seated in their vicinity. Early theatres such as London's 16th century 'Globe' had balconies supported on heavy wooden pillars. By the 19th and early 20th centuries, iron was used as this was stronger, and so pillars could be less bulky and intrusive. Clearly, an advance such as this, which avoids the need for pillars at all, is a huge step forward. Concrete also became a popular material for theatre and cinema interiors because it was resistant to fire and could be moulded to create elaborate shapes for decoration.

2.10 Hebden Bridge Picture House balcony, Sarah Mason Photography

The formal opening ceremony of the new building took place on 12th July 1921. Mr Fredrick Cockcroft, Chairman of the Directors of the Picture House, welcomed the guests and visitors before the cinema was formally opened by Mrs. Cockcroft. She said that she had great pleasure in declaring the Picture House open and wished it every success. The Chairman of the Urban District Council, Mr George Atack J.P., congratulated the Directors on providing for the inhabitants of Hebden Bridge 'a magnificent place of entertainment'.

At the end of the ceremony a portrait of King George was shown on the screen, the audience standing and singing the National Anthem accompanied by the orchestra. The cinema then showed a selection of travel and topical pictures, followed by a musical programme played by a quartet comprising a violin played by Miss Martha Ingham, a

31

flute played by Mr. Jenkinson, a violin-cello by Mr. Walter Ashworth, and a piano played by Mr. T.G.Wild.

The Hebden Bridge Times and Caldervale Gazette covered the event:

"'A fine place' was the general verdict of those who were privileged to attend the opening of the new Picture House in New Road, Hebden Bridge last Monday afternoon. Convenience, comfort, and elegance are the features which impress the visitor as he enters and takes his seat. He feels that he could sit a long time in that sort of easy-chair without being tired, and the upholstery is of a pleasing old-gold colour. The coming of other patrons does not disturb him, for the floor-covering - carpet in the aisles, cork lino for the remainder - is sufficiently thick to neutralise the sound of footsteps. The hall is tastefully decorated in a quiet unobtrusive scheme of fawn and white panels, with a delightful brown shade for the lower part of the walls, the moulding being light and artistic. And as the lights are turned down and the programme is gone through the visitor speedily becomes aware of other advantages - of the noiselessness of the projector and the steadiness of the screen pictures; and of the acoustic qualities of the hall, which make all the more enjoyable the music played by a capable orchestra, and enable a speaker on the platform to be heard distinctly. Further, as one is seated, there is a clear view of the screen or platform to be had, without craning the neck or leaning to one side to see round the person in front. These are good features in a hall which, apart from its use primarily as a picture house, may occasionally in the future be used for large public meetings, concerts etc.

From the first, one is impressed by the steady projection, the clear focus, and absence of noise. There is no flickering whatsoever and one could not help comparing this favourable feature with what one had to put up with in the early days of cinema when the wavering and fluttering of the picture on the screen gave one a decided eye strain. As a picture show it was entirely satisfactory, and the quietude and comfort helped one to enjoy it to the full."

In the early days of cinema a selection of short films was usually shown, each perhaps only a few minutes long. By the 1920's however, feature films had arrived. The first films shown at the new Picture House were 'Torn Sails' and 'The Iron Stair'.

'Torn Sails' (1920) is a drama directed by A.V.Bramble and starring Milton Rosmer, Mary Odette and Geoffrey Kerr. It was based on the 1897 novel 'Torn Sails' by Allen Raine. The film is set in a small Welsh village and is the story of a woman who weds a man she doesn't love. He then dies in a fire set by another woman.

2.11(left) Mary Odette, star of 'Torn Sails', Copyright Ideal Film Company 1920
2.12 (right) Milton Rosmer, star of 'Torn Sails, Copyright Ideal Film Company 1920

'The Iron Stair' (1920) is a British crime drama directed by F. Martin Thornton from the novel 'The Iron Stair' by Rita (the pen-name of prolific British author, Eliza Margaret Jane Humphreys (née Gollan)). It is a tale of twin brothers, one of whom forges a cheque which results in the other brother going to prison. The first brother then repents and swaps places with his brother in prison. A warder rumbles the brothers' plot and the situation soon escalates into murder and suicide. The film starred Reginald Fox and Madge Stuart.

2.13 Still from "The Iron Stair', Copyright Stoll Film Company 1920

On the first weekend after opening the Picture House showed as the principal film, 'Anna, The Adventuress'. Here we see another story involving identical siblings who swap places, this time sisters. This film was directed by Cecil Hepworth and starred Alma Taylor, Jean Cadell and James Carew. It was based on a novel by E. Phillips Oppenheim. This film was described in the local newspaper at the time as 'a fine Hepworth film'.

2.14 (left) Alma Taylor, star of 'Anna The Adventuress'', Copyright Hepworth Picture Plays, 1920
2.15 (right) Cecil Hepworth, director, Public Domain

Competition for film audiences in Hebden Bridge was still strong and that weekend the Co-op Hall cinema competed with the film 'The Beloved Cheater', which was reported in the press as 'an almost perfect comedy'.

Despite this competition the Picture House went from strength to strength, soon becoming the main place of entertainment for the weavers, mill workers, and residents of the Upper Calder Valley. Incidentally, the cinema at the Co-op Hall was to close down in 1930 with the advent of talking pictures.

For those visiting the Picture House at this time the price of the front seats was six pence, the rest of the stalls cost one shilling, and the balcony one shilling and six pence. Children were charged half the adult price. In decimal currency that would be two and a half pence, five pence, and approximately eight pence.

In 1924, the Dramatic Sub-Section of the Hebden Bridge Literary & Scientific Society was formed. Their first play, 'The Walls of Jericho' was performed at the Co-op Hall on the 18th December. Their dramatic work was well-received by the townspeople of Hebden Bridge. By 1928, they were putting on three plays a year and attracting large audiences. In that year they transferred to the Picture House for their performances. They were charged £40 for the hire of the cinema for three nights. In the late 1920's and 1930's, the Literary & Scientific Society also hired the Picture House for their monthly lectures. One regular speaker was coal merchant, Joe Bradley, who was also a well known cyclist. He gave entertaining lectures about his cycling adventures. Thus began the Picture House's 'alter-ego' life as a live entertainment venue as well as a cinema.

2.16 New Road 1931, facade of Picture House can be seen on the right, postcard image courtesy of Paul Haywood, Copyright Mr S L Smith

So in 1921, when the doors of the Picture House swung open for the first time and the townspeople of Hebden Bridge entered the grand cinema, built with so much post-war optimism and pride, how advanced was the film industry and how strong a player was Britain in it?

At the beginning of the twentieth century, Britain's film industry was thriving and many film studios were set up, mainly around London. In the 1920's, however, U.S. film production took off with the establishment of large studios there, particularly in Hollywood.

The U.S. film director, D.W. Griffith, was one of the first to see the advantages of the west coast of America as a base for film production. He began filming in Hollywood around 1910. In the years that followed, other film-makers, hearing of Griffith's success, followed him there to set up their own studios. There were several important factors which encouraged this choice of location. The weather in California was more reliable for year-round filming and the scenery was very varied over a relatively small area. Also, at this time, Thomas Edison who was based on the east coast of the U.S., held many patents relating to film-making technology. He and his 'Motion Picture Patents Company' held a monopoly on film-making. There have even been allegations that the 'Mob' was used to 'enforce' these patents at times! Judges on the West Coast tended to be less friendly to Edison and it was a long way for law enforcement agents (or mobsters!) from the East Coast to travel.

These Hollywood studios were producing glamorous, expensive, heavily marketed feature films against which British film-makers found it hard to compete. Indeed, by 1926, only 5% of films shown in UK cinemas were British-made. The biggest star of the silent era, British comedian Charlie Chaplin, starred in films made in Hollywood.

2.17 Charlie Chaplin, Keystone Studios - Public Domain

In 1927, the British Government recognised the importance of film production to the U.K. economy and acted to protect the U.K. market from American domination by means of the Cinematograph Films Act 1927. This stated that cinemas must show a certain percentage of British films to encourage U.K. film production. The Act was a success in that production of films in Britain more than doubled by the end of the decade. Conversely, however, it also created a market for poor quality, low cost films, made in order to satisfy the quota - the 'quota quickies' as they became known.

Film studios were also being set up in other parts of the world at this time. The European silent film industry, known as 'The Other Hollywood' included movements such as German Expressionism, Soviet Montage, French Impressionism, Poetic Realism and Italian Neorealism.

3. Sound Progress

"Film as dream, film as music. No art passes our conscience in the way film does, and goes directly to our feelings, deep down into the twilight rooms of our souls."
Ingmar Bergman (6)

A significant milestone in the history of film-making was the arrival of the 'talkies' (films with sound). Occurring around 1928, this was actually of great benefit to the British film industry because, unlike the films from France and Germany, those from Britain could compete in the American market without being dubbed. The industry boomed, alliances were forged with U.S. companies and film production began to increase. In Britain in the early 1930's, new cinemas were being built and cinema as a form of entertainment was thriving.

The Technicolor film process was also a major advance at this time. It was invented in 1916 and gradually improved so that, by the late 1930's, it could be used on feature films. Although the majority of films in this era were still made in monochrome, films in colour had started to appear. 'Snow White and the Seven Dwarfs' was released in the U.K. in March 1938. Soon afterwards, when it was screened at the Picture House, the locals crowded in to see it. It was the first feature film to appear in colour and would have been a lively topic of conversation in the town. Over the next couple of years, 'The Wizard of Oz' and 'Gone With The Wind' colour films also appeared.

Britain's cinema scene became dominated by three large cinema chains around this time - Associated British Cinemas (ABC), Gaumont and Odeon. Between them, these companies operated almost a thousand cinemas. Small independent cinemas, such as Hebden Bridge Picture House, would have found it difficult to vie for the most popular films early after their release against such competition - a challenge for small cinemas which persists to this day.

3.1 Still from Snow White and the Seven Dwarfs, 1937, Copyright Disney

3.2 Judy Garland in 'The Wizard of Oz', 1939, Copyright MGM Studios

When war was declared in 1939, all cinemas, including the Picture House, were closed down. They were opened again, however, after about a week, as the authorities appreciated how important they would be for morale and to communicate news.

Despite the hardships and restrictions of war, the British cinema industry actually continued to rally. Films were produced, for example 'In Which We Serve', 'First of the Few' and 'One of our Aircraft is Missing', depicting the struggles, turmoils and triumphs of war. Cinema attendances in Britain rose to an all-time high of 1,635 million visits in 1946, as these morale-boosting films captured the imagination of the public.

Audiences at the Picture House were also able to escape from the weariness of the war years, enjoying a series of elaborate Hollywood musicals made around this time. These included 'Anchors Aweigh', featuring Frank Sinatra in his first major role. A host of other stars also emerged including Judy Garland, Fred Astaire, Humphrey Bogart, Bob Hope and Ingrid Bergman.

3.3 Fred Astaire in 'You'll Never Get Rich' (1941), Public Domain

41

3.4 (left) Ingrid Bergman, c.1942, Public Domain
3.5 (right) Humphrey Bogart, 1940, Public Domain

3.6 Bob Hope entertains the troops in WWII, Public Domain

On Wednesday 27th June 1945, as part of his pre-election tour of West Yorkshire, Winston Churchill visited Hebden Bridge. As Mr Churchill's entourage drove through the Calder Valley people gathered at the sides of the road, cheering. A woman in Mytholmroyd broke free of the throng and pressed a cigar into his hands. Mr Churchill stood at the front of the car acknowledging the crowd by waving his arms and his hat and giving his famous 'V' sign as he arrived into Hebden Bridge. New Road, from Crown Street to Hope Street, was packed with people as he stood in front of the Picture House to speak to the crowd:

"You played a great part during the war and the name of Britain stood very high all over the world. We were respected for the way we stood alone and for the great deeds of our armies in many different parts of the world, and for what we did on the sea and in the air. We bear a good name; let us make sure by pulling together, sticking together and pressing onwards with social reform, we remain, whether in war or in peace, a nation respected, honoured and in the forefront of the victorious nations of the world."

After his speech he received three cheers from the crowd and then, flourishing a 'V' sign, he continued on his way to Todmorden.

3.7 Churchill arrives at Hebden Bridge, junction of New Road and Commercial Street, 1945, Alice Longstaff Gallery Collection

3.8 Churchill addresses the crowds outside the Picture House, 1945, M. Sunderland, Hebden Bridge Local History Society

3.9 Churchill near the New Olympia cinema, Todmorden, 1945, Todmorden Antiquarian Society

44

Developments in film-making continued. Improved sound, special effects and clever photography meant that films had become easier to watch. CinemaScope, a method of shooting and then projecting wide-screen films, was developed in 1952. Advances such as these helped to maintain the attraction of the cinema, and the Picture House entertained large audiences throughout the 1940's and early 1950's.

We see Hebden Bridge Picture House flourishing during this time, maintaining its place as one of the main entertainment venues in town. The local newspaper advertised which films were showing and, in many households, a visit to the cinema at least once a week was part of the fabric of life. As a result, the Picture House rarely lacked a large audience.

Among the locals who enjoyed visiting the Picture House around this time were Molly Sunderland and her sister, Josephine. Molly tells us that she and her sister used to sit in the 'cheap seats' at the front of the cinema. Tickets for these seats were sold from a small kiosk just inside the side door to the left of the screen, and the people queued along the side of the cinema waiting for the doors to open. The first four or five rows of seats were separated from the rest by ropes across the aisles. Molly remembers that the lads would often find better seats by ducking under the rope once the film had started if the usherette was not on watch!

Occasionally, on Sunday evenings, as a change from film screenings, live entertainment was provided at the Picture House. For example, a 'Celebrity Concert' was hosted by the cinema in October, 1945. It featured contralto Kathleen Ferrier, supported by other well-known musicians and vocalists, and a choir. The Hebden Bridge Times reviewed this concert. They reported that the artistes gave splendid performances but the programme lacked variety in the selection of vocal pieces. The newspaper also said that the choir contributed numerous part-songs under the able leadership of Mr J. W. Lingard, and their singing was well-appreciated.

HEBDEN, BOYD AND HEPTON HOSPITAL APPEAL
COMMITTEE (Musical Section).

CELEBRITY CONCERT

PICTURE HOUSE, HEBDEN BRIDGE,
SUNDAY, 21st OCTOBER, 1945.

Special Engagement of First Class Artistes:

KATHLEEN FERRIER, Contralto.
DAVID LLOYD, Tenor.
JACK MACKINTOSH, Trumpet.
ALBERT HARDIE, Accompanist.

3.10 Advertisment for the 'Celebrity Concert', Hebden Bridge Times

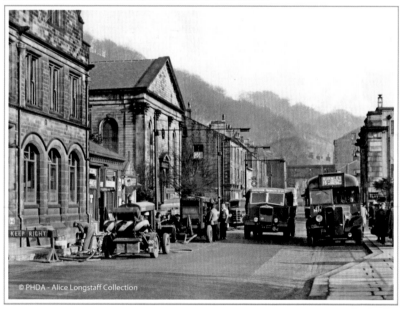

© PHDA - Alice Longstaff Collection

3.11 New Road, Hebden Bridge, 1950, Picture House visible on right, Alice Longstaff Gallery Collection

46

Films showing at the cinema were changed twice a week. They were delivered to the cinema by station van, having arrived into Hebden Bridge by train. The cinema manager walked to the station once a week to pay for delivery and he always had a couple of free cinema tickets for the staff. Reportedly, these tickets only reached the junior station staff if the films that week were thought to be 'not very interesting'!

3.12 (above) Hebden Bridge station, 1950's, Donald Taylor Collection
3.13 (below) Hebden Bridge station, 1951, Lancashire & Yorkshire Railway Society

In 1951, Star Cinemas took over the running of the Picture House from Thistle Holme Estate Company. They produced a plan of the auditorium (below), which shows just how many extra rows of seats there were at that time. Imagine how cramped the seating would have been compared to the ample leg-room enjoyed nowadays!

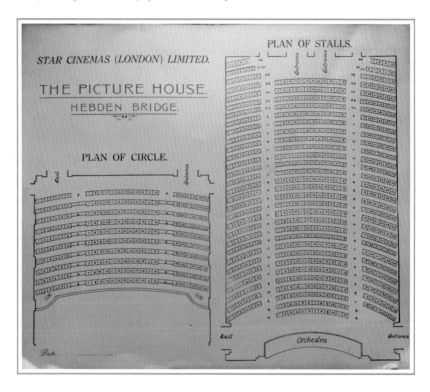

3.14 Plan of Picture House auditorium produced by Star Cinemas, Picture House Archives

After this change in management and because other cinemas in the area opened on Sundays, application was made for Sunday opening. By law at this time, Sunday opening was only permitted if a local poll voted in favour of it. A public meeting took place in Hebden Bridge during which there must have been much argument. When the meeting voted, 175

48

were against Sunday opening and only 48 were in favour of it. There followed a protest and, to make sure that voting was more representative of the town, the council organised an official poll. This resulted in 1130 votes in favour of Sunday opening and 1156 against. Five years later, in October 1956, another poll produced 1225 votes in favour of Sunday opening and 777 against. That settled the matter: Sunday opening was approved.

Also introduced in this era, Saturday matinee shows for children immediately became very popular. The children enjoyed them, the parents knew they were safe and, of course, the cinemas were trying to ingrain the habit of cinema-going from a young age! Local film-goer, Tom Greenwood remembers the Saturday matinees:

"There would be a serial every week which would end on a cliffhanger. There was one called 'Captain Marvel' and another one was 'The Perils of Nyoka'. We used to cheer, 'The Goodies are coming!' If you were too noisy they used to shine a torch at you as a warning and, if you carried on, you'd be told to leave.

The manager was called Eric and he used to wear a dark suit. If the film broke the children would stamp their feet and call for Eric to fix it. Eric would stand up on stage and announce that there was a problem with the film but he always managed to fix it so that we could see the end.

The local lads used to go to the Picture House to smoke and, of course, if you had a girl friend you'd take her there.

I remember all the schools were taken to the Picture House to see the coronation in 1953. The place was packed and everyone was cheering. There was also a special showing for schools to see the film of the first ascent of Everest. I remember that there was lots of footage of the base-camp and the preparations for the climb but there was no footage of the top of the mountain, just a still photo of Edmund Hilary disappearing into the snow!"

3.15 (left) Nyoka, 1946, Public Domain
3.16 (right) Captain Marvel, 1941, Public Domain

In 1951, we also see the opening of the Festival of Britain, a national exhibition held on the South Bank of the Thames in London. The aim was to promote Britain's contribution to science, technology, industry and the arts, and to boost recovery from the effects of war in these fields. Newsreels at Hebden Bridge Picture House would have provided glimpses of the Dome of Discovery, the iconic Skylon and other exciting exhibitions. One feature at the Festival was a 400 seat state-of-the-art cinema equipped to screen not only films, but large screen television broadcasts. Perhaps an omen of challenging times ahead for cinema?

Unfortunately for the Picture House, the latter half of the 1950's did indeed welcome in new avenues of home entertainment such as television and radio. Television became more popular, particularly after the coronation of Queen Elizabeth II was televised in 1953. This was, predictably, reflected in a downturn in the fortune of the film industry, many studios being forced to close down as the decade progressed. Cinema audiences also fell as homes became more comfortable and entertainment at home more readily available.

Hebden Bridge Picture House also began to suffer at this time due to the changes in fortune of the town itself. During the 1940's and early 1950's, the local textile industry flourished. People had money to spend on entertainment and the Picture House benefitted. Around 1960, however, major changes were taking place. Overseas markets were developing their own textile industries and man-made fibres were more readily available. This affected the demand for cotton mills. Many mills and factories in Hebden Bridge had to close down. Unemployment rose in the town, the townspeople had less disposable income and many left to look for work elsewhere. As the 1960's dawned, this depression was felt by the Picture House as cinema audiences began to shrink. Challenging times were to come, as we will see in the next chapter. Before we move on with our story, however, here are two first-hand accounts of life at the Picture House at this time.

Peter Copley, a local resident, remembers with fondness Saturday mornings at the Picture House:

"Todmorden, where I was born, had three cinemas - the Olympia, the Hippodrome and the Gem up Cornholme, but it was the Saturday matinees at the Picture House that I have the fondest memories of. At the age of seven or eight, I would travel from Tod to Hebden Bridge by bus. I think the bus fare was 3d (three old pence.) I would travel either with my sister, school pals or even alone, as was the way of the day. Parents would be happy in the knowledge that their children would be safe in the warm friendly cinema.

I remember, it must have been around 1952 or 1953, just at the time sweets were coming off ration, 3d would buy 2oz of caramels. One day, instead of coming home on the bus, I decided to spend my bus fare on sweets and walk home. There were no more than four or five toffees in the bag and by the time I'd walked to the top of Bridge Lane I'd finished them. I never realised how far a four-mile hike is to a 9 year-old!

The matinees started around 1pm and finished around 3.30pm. There was always a cartoon, an episode from a serial and then the main film, usually a 'Cowboy' film. Often, the film projector would break down mid-film, triggering five hundred boys and girls to begin a spontaneous drum-beat of feet stamping until the film was fixed!

During the interval, children whose birthday it was during that week, were invited up onto the stage. The MC asked the same question each week: 'What do you want to be when you grow up?' The boys usually answered that they wanted to be a fireman or a train driver or now and then, something else but the girls always answered that they wanted to be a nurse.

On my way home from the cinema, no matter how hard I tried, I could never see a way out of the dangerous predicament that Dick Barton, Special Agent or Flash Gordon was put in by the villains - such as being tied up in a room that was filling with water. There was no way out and surely they must drown or come to some other sticky end! I looked forward all week to finding out what happened next.

You could always tell what type of picture had been showing by the action of the kids as they streamed out of the pictures - either sword fencing with pretend swords or pointed fingers shooting guns or drawing invisible bows and firing off arrows at a rate that would have done justice to the longbow men at Agincourt!"

Ann Hawkes worked as an usherette at the Picture House from 1960 to 1962. She gives us a fascinating snapshot of life in and around the cinema at that time:

"I remember a couple, Eric and Joyce, ran the Picture House. I started work in the sewing shop at a quarter to eight in the morning, and finished at a quarter past five in the afternoon. Then I went to the Picture House to work evenings.

Joyce would leave me some sandwiches to eat before I started work.

Films were shown there every evening and there were three shows on a Saturday - a kids' show in the morning, an afternoon matinee and an evening show. The films were changed on a Thursday and a Sunday. The kids' show started with a cartoon, then a serial which always ended on a cliffhanger, then a kids' film. The children all came to the cinema on their own on Saturday morning, they were all ages in the queue outside, from five years up.

The ticket counter was at the bottom of the stairs next to the doors into the auditorium. Joyce would sit there and sell tickets and an usherette would stand between the doors to the auditorium to tear the tickets and put the stubs on a string as the people went in. The sweet kiosk was where it is now. It sold cans of pop, chocolate and crisps.

There would be two usherettes, one for downstairs and one for upstairs, but on Saturdays, when it was busier, there would be three, two downstairs and one up. You needed extra staff on a Saturday when the kids came for the matinees....they usually behaved themselves, though, because they knew I knew their mother! Everyone knew everyone then.

There was a B-film and then an A-film and films were much shorter in those days. There were two seats at the back of the stalls, near the ladies' toilets, where we sat during the film. I saw lots of films but we never got to see the beginnings or ends of them! The films were on big reels and the projectionist had to watch for the dots to warn him to change the reel. The films rarely broke but when they did, the people were very good-natured. They would shout, 'Put a shilling in the meter!' or something like that. At the interval, we had to change into white tabards to sell ice-creams. We stood at the front on the left of the screen under the clock to do this.

The upstairs was always open and there was usually a good turn-out for the shows. I remember when we showed 'Whistle Down The Wind', the queue stretched all the way

53

down the road and round the corner to the Post Office. I didn't think we would get them all in but we did. There were lots more seats then, of course, and much closer together. When you sat down, your knees touched the seat in front. The tall men used to sit on the ends of rows to stick their legs out. I remember that there were double seats at the front on both sides of the balcony. The cinema was popular with courting couples because you were away from your family but it was respectable.

The screen was much smaller then than it is now and, of course, everyone was smoking so it was like walking through a fog in there! After the show we had to put gloves on and clean out the ash-trays before we finished work."

3.17 School children visit the Picture House c.1964, Picture House Archives

3.18 Picture House foyer c.1965, note ticket booth position at the bottom of the stairs, Picture House Archives

55

4. Dark Days

"The public has lost the habit of movie-going because the cinema no longer possesses the charm, the hypnotic charisma, the authority it once commanded. The image it once held for us all - that of a dream we dreamt with our eyes open - has disappeared. Is it still possible that one thousand people might group together in the dark and experience the dream that a single individual has directed?"
Federico Fellini (7)

During the early 1960's, Hebden Bridge was in decline. Many of the mills were closing, some of the factories and shops lay empty or derelict and many of the townspeople had had to move elsewhere to find work. This, together with the national decline in cinema audiences due to the arrival of other more accessible forms of entertainment such as television, meant that the Picture House was entering a perilous period indeed.

4.1 New Road, Hebden Bridge, c.1960, Picture House just visible on right, Alice Longstaff Gallery Collection

Generally, cinemas were operated by companies as commercial enterprises to produce profits for shareholders. As audiences dwindled many of the larger cinemas sub-divided their single auditorium into two or three smaller screens. In this way they could keep popular films for longer to get as much profit from them as possible. Those unfortunate cinemas which failed to make a profit were closed down, often converting to bingo halls.

In 1964, the now run-down, old fashioned, loss-making Picture House was closed down for several months. Our story could have ended here but for the arrival of cinema fanatic, Lloyd Brearley. He believed that the Picture House should have a future so he and a business partner made the brave move of purchasing the building outright.

By now, a young man named Roger Bogg had also joined the team. Over the next forty years or so, he was to become a well-known stalwart of the Picture House and a much loved and loyal projectionist.

Audience numbers were down, money was tight and the outlook for the Picture House was bleak. Lloyd and his small team ran the cinema on a shoe string. He helped operate the film projectors while his wife cleaned the auditorium. In the intervals between films, cinema-goers were entertained with recordings of Glenn Miller, played on a 78 rpm record player.

Lloyd battled on in this way for the next few years, his belief in the Picture House unshakeable. Sadly, however, by 1971, the cinema had become such a financial liability that he was forced to sell it.

We will have the opportunity to learn more about Lloyd Brearley and life at the Picture House during these difficult years at the end of this chapter, when we hear from Graham Cobham, whose family were closely involved with the cinema around this time.

4.2 Lloyd Brearley, photograph courtesy of Martin Parr, © Martin Parr / Magnum Photos

The building came very close to being sold off as a carpet warehouse but, at the last minute, the chairman of Council Planning, David Fletcher, proposed that the Picture House be purchased as a local amenity. This was approved and it was bought by Hebden Royd Urban District Council for the sum of £6,500. The decision for the Council to buy the Picture House was in spite of strong opposition from a number of councillors who foresaw that unending financial support would be necessary to maintain the cinema. One councillor resigned in protest.

Following the Council's purchase of the cinema, Lloyd Brearley was able to stay on as manager, still determined that the Picture House should not close down. Sadly, however, the decline continued and later that year the cinema was threatened with closure again. Lloyd once more showed his passionate belief in the Picture House by speaking to the people of Hebden Bridge and organising a petition for its reprieve. Within a week of starting the petition he had collected almost a thousand signatures. Because of this the closure was shelved.

By 1973, the Council, realising quite how much financial support the ailing Picture House needed, put forward a plan to convert the building into a 'multi-purpose centre'. It would have provision for a small cinema, a large sports hall and other facilities. These plans (see 4.3 & 4.4 below) were put forward at a public meeting and the cost was estimated at about £60,000.

The fate of the Picture House hung in the balance once again but, as luck would have it, in the local government reorganisation of 1974, the cinema was transferred to the ownership of the new Calderdale Metropolitan Council. In this new organisation the plans to convert it into a multi-purpose building were not prioritised. The Picture House lived on to fight another day.

59

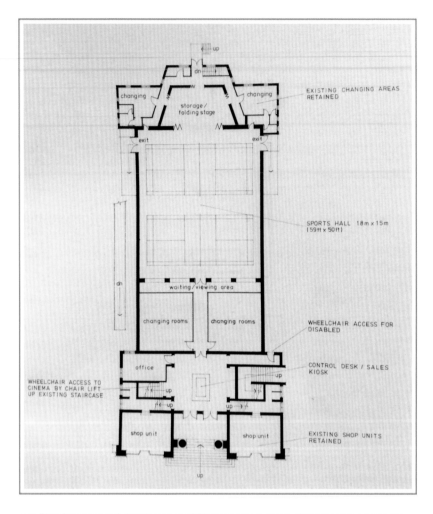

4.3 Plan for proposed development of Picture House, 1973, Picture House Archives

60

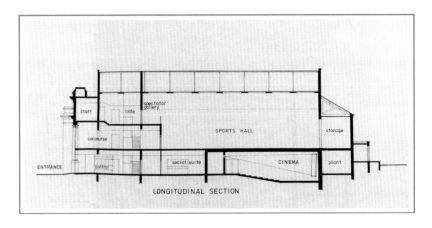

4.4 Plan for proposed development of the Picture House, 1973, Picture House Archives

In January 1975, a Council Recreations and Amenities Committee carried out a review of buildings under their control as part of a cost cutting exercise. The Picture House and the Civic Hall in Hebden Bridge (now the Crown Inn) came under scrutiny. A report showed that the cost of maintaining the Civic Hall was much higher than that of maintaining the cinema. It also concluded that the cinema was more likely to be of use as a local amenity and the decision was taken to close down the Civic Hall rather than the Picture House. Once again the future of the Picture House had hung by a thread and once again it survived. Hebden Bridge Picture House seemed to be teetering from one cliffhanger ending to another, reminiscent of the Saturday morning serials of its heyday!

Following the decision to close the Civic Hall and to spare the Picture House, the Council then agreed to spend £24,000 on improvements to the cinema which had become rather shabby and dilapidated. The council hoped that these measures would attract more patrons and result in the cinema paying its way.

4.5 Civic Hall, Crown Street, Hebden Bridge, 2016, now The Crown Inn, Kate Higham

Despite these efforts, however, attendances continued to drop. A few months later the cinema was forced to close for two days every week in a bid to cut the continuing losses. The Picture House's future was in doubt again as its position became ever more precarious.

A financial report commissioned recommended that the cinema be sold off. However, in a bold forward-thinking move, the Council decided otherwise and, in 1977, a £50,000 scheme to renovate the building and improve stage facilities went ahead. It was hoped that it would continue in its major role as a cinema but that it would be better equipped for other live events and for use by local groups and societies, thus providing another income stream. The aim was that, as fuller use of the building was made, future financial support would be reduced.

4.6 Hebden Bridge Picture House, 1976, Hebden Bridge Camera Club

It was at the time of this refurbishment that Chief Administration Officer, Michael Scott, said that although the building bore the name 'Hebden Bridge Picture House', it was usually referred to as 'Hebden Bridge Cinema' so its name should be changed appropriately. The Picture House was the Picture House no more. During the renovations, a new sign bearing the name 'Hebden Bridge Cinema' was erected over the front doors.

The stone work was cleaned, the roof was repaired, re-wiring was carried out and the heating system renovated. A new slide-away cinema screen was installed and the building was completely re-decorated. The stage was improved and new dressing rooms were provided. The 690 seats were removed from the stalls and replaced by just 257. This provided the much-praised extra leg room between the seats which is still one of the talking points of the cinema nowadays! The seats in the balcony were unaltered and remained rather cramped and uncomfortable. The re-wiring of the building's electrics resulted in the replacement of the 29 flickering gas lamps which lit the building. Prior to this, it had been the task of one of the staff to go round with a taper to light up all of these lamps before the public could be allowed into the building.

4.7 Visit to the Picture House by the Mayor of Calderdale, 1977, Hebden Bridge Camera Club

Following the refurbishment, the re-opening festivities began on Sunday 30th April 1978, when the cinema was opened for public viewing. This was followed by a week of stage shows organised by the Hebden Bridge Light Opera Society. On Monday, the week began with a 'Sit Down and Sing' concert by the Hebden Bridge Junior Band, which was recorded by Radio Leeds for broadcast at a later date. Hebden Bridge Light Opera Society contributed with their presentation of 'Half A Sixpence'. Halifax Male Voice Choir, Sowerby Bridge Gilbert & Sullivan Society, Hebden Bridge Little Theatre and St. Michael's Amateur Operatic Society were among the other organisations that appeared on stage. At the end of the week, on Sunday 7th May, the James Bond film, 'The Spy Who loved Me' was screened.

Manager, Lloyd Brearley, was jubilant that finally money was being spent on the cinema. He hoped that this would entice local people through the doors once again and help to regain the cinema's position as one of the main entertainment venues in Hebden Bridge. He said that the face lift made a vast improvement and it was marvellous that a town the size of Hebden Bridge could have a cinema when other much larger towns could not keep one going.

This mood of optimism was reflected in the rest of Hebden Bridge around this time. Following a massive clean-up operation, the town was starting to see an influx of new residents. The first of these became known as the 'Hebden Bridge Hippies'. These would be followed by artists, musicians, alternative practitioners and then young professionals from Leeds and Manchester - no doubt tempted by the low property prices. The result would be a town where many different cultures came together to produce a community which was arty, bohemian, creative, positive and forward-thinking.

Calderdale Public Halls Manager, David Hird, hoped that the cinema would become 'Calderdale's second theatre'. He announced that one of the first events planned would be an exhibition, talk and demonstration by Yorkshire artist, Ashley Jackson.

The cinema did go on to host many more live events successfully over the next few years. These included a folk concert, a jazz evening, a fashion show, theatrical shows and a disco. One play with music was called 'Taking Our Time'. It was based on the industrialisation of the weaving industry in Yorkshire and the rise of Chartism.

Very sadly, in November 1981, after many years of loyal service, Mr Lloyd Brearley died. He was succeeded as manager by Mr Maurice Robson. Mr Robson had been fascinated by cinema all his life. During the war, he had used a hand-turned projector to put on films for children at his home.

His first job, on leaving school in 1945, was at the Victoria Hall Cinema in Halifax (now the Civic Theatre). In 1957, Mr Robson was projectionist at the Palladium in Elland, after which he became manager of the Savoy Cinema in Huddersfield. From 1969 to 1980 he owned and ran a record shop in Elland but then, in 1982, he returned to his first love - the cinema.

4.8 Maurice Robson, 1981, Hebden BridgeTimes

Maurice, his team at Hebden Bridge Cinema and the Council clearly had hopes for a brighter, more financially secure future as the 1980's progressed. Sadly, however, this did not materialise. Despite the refurbishment and the broader appeal of the building for hosting live events, attendances failed to increase, the cinema was as big a money drain as ever and further significant financial support was necessary. Its future was again seriously threatened.

4.9 Maurice Robson with members of the Picture House team, Picture House Archives

On a national level, Hebden Bridge Cinema was not alone in experiencing these difficulties. Film production in Britain declined during the 1980's. The incoming Thatcher government removed some of the financial support for the film industry and tightened tax rules for film-makers. Cinema audiences continued to decline due to improvement in television, the choice of more television channels and the advent of video. In fact, the annual attendance at British cinemas for 1984 was an all-time low at 54 million.

In 1983, in response to a request by Calderdale Metropolitan Council, Hebden Bridge Town Council assessed the options for the cinema's future. They suggested that it should be converted into a multi-purpose building similar to that suggested in 1973. This would accommodate a large sports hall and a small cinema. In the Council's opinion the combined package could be financially viable and the town would still have access to film entertainment. David Hird, however, said that it would signal the end of 'big' films in Hebden Bridge because film distributors would not be prepared to release copies for small audiences.

Despite these arguments, Calderdale accepted the Town Council's suggestion to convert the building in this way. However, in the 1984 budget, the Council granted another temporary reprieve and allowed enough money to pay for the running costs for another year in the first instance. The fate of the cinema was uncertain but, again, it appeared to be under a stay of execution.

As if this was not challenging enough, the arrival of the first multiplex in 1985 signalled the advent of a further threat to the survival of small independent cinemas. A leisure centre was built in Milton Keynes which incorporated a ten screen cinema. It was designed and operated by a U.S. company and was an immediate success, recording over one million admissions in its first year of business. This paved the way for many more multiplexes to spring up all over the country. These were usually built out of town with ample free parking and food outlets on-site. Traditional town and city-centre cinemas were unable to compete with this and, sadly, many more of them began to close down.

4.10 The Point multiplex cinema, Milton Keynes, Copyright Harry Rigby and licenced for re-use under this Creative Commons (Attribution) License - http:// cinematreasures.org/ theaters/25085/photos/ 111079

Over the next few years Hebden Bridge Cinema did continue to operate, although still perilously close to closure. With each crisis it would seem that there was no way out - but each time someone would step up or fate would take a hand to allow this town treasure just one more chance......

In June 1987, Calderdale Council considered a suggestion by the newly formed Hebden Bridge Festival Theatre Company that the cinema could be converted to an 'Arts & Media Centre'. The idea was to establish a professional theatre in Calderdale allowing Hebden Bridge to develop as a theatrical venue of national standing. After a feasibility study, however, the idea was abandoned.

In 1986/7, Leeds polytechnic students carried out a survey in the Hebden Bridge area on future uses for the cinema building. Calderdale's analysis of their results indicated that the local community would be happy to see it remain as a cinema. However, it did throw up the rather bizarre suggestion from some people that the building could be used as a nuclear shelter! A sign of the times, perhaps.

On a national level, cinema attendance was actually picking up due to the success of the multiplexes. John Major's government was more concerned about the future of the British film industry. The British Film Commission was set up, some tax relief was granted to film-makers and a proportion of Lottery money was also allocated to the film industry. The future for British cinema began to seem a little brighter.

12th July 1991 marked the 70th anniversary of the opening of Hebden Bridge Picture House. The celebrations began on the Sunday evening with a floating reception on the canal boat, 'Sarah Siddons', moored at the rear of the cinema. It was attended by the Mayor of Calderdale, Councillor Tom McElroy, and the Mayor of Hebden Bridge, Councillor Peter Horne.

Mr. Robson hoped that older film-goers would enjoy seeing favourites such as Al Jolson in 'The Singing Fool' and Errol Flynn in 'The Sea Hawk' once again on a full-sized cinema screen. To see a matinee performance of one of the most famous of all films, 'Gone With The Wind', film buffs paid the original 1920's price, six pence (old money). Pensioners who celebrated their 70th birthday during July were admitted free.

4.11 Programme for seventieth anniversary screenings, Picture House Archives

Throughout the week the cinema screened a selection of films made during the life of the cinema. The celebrations started with Al Jolson in 'The Singing Fool' from 1928. Other classic films included British War time hit, 'Way To The Stars', with Michael Redgrave and John Mills, Dirk Bogard's 1958 'Tale of Two Cities', swashbuckling Errol Flynn in 'The Sea Hawk', Kenneth Moore in 'Genevieve' and Sam playing it again in 'Casablanca'. The week concluded on Saturday with 'Gone With The Wind'.

Maurice Robson was quoted as saying:

"The Picture House has seen some remarkable changes since that opening night and has entertained thousands of local people. With so many of our older cinemas closing down, we think that having seen 70 years in business and still going strong is something to celebrate."

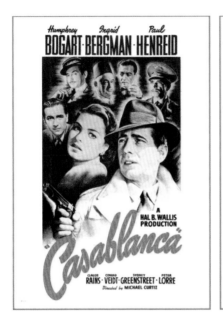 

4.12 (left) 'Casablanca', 1942, original movie poster, Public Domain
4.13 (right) 'Gone With The Wind', 1939, original movie poster, Public Domain

Things finally seemed to be improving for the cinema. In 1996, the main stairs and auditorium were re-decorated and fire doors fitted to the stalls and balcony.

Later that year, however, cuts in the budget for public spending forced Calderdale Council to slash its £16,000 subsidy of the cinema. The Council's Leisure Services Committee met to discuss how they could seek an independent operator to lease and run it. They stipulated that whoever took on this lease must comply with the Council's

policies regarding film programming and customer care. The tender process did not, however, yield any serious private sector interest, leaving the Council with three options:
- to sell the cinema
- to lease it with no control over programming, customer care etc.
- to retain the cinema as a public amenity.

The option to sell off the building was thoroughly explored over the next few months. A report advised the Council that if it were to be put on the market, subject to a condition that it remain as a cinema, it should be advertised requesting offers in the region of £65,000. The report also said that 'the majority of this value would be the fact that the owner would benefit from the income from the shop lettings'. It went on to say that if it were to be sold without these conditions then demolition to make way for a smaller building with parking in front would be a likely outcome. In this case, it would fetch around £80,000.

Dark days indeed, and another seemingly hopeless situation, another moment when the cinema's future hung by a thread. However, they say that 'a friend in need is a friend indeed' and this was about to be well and truly put to the test.

Several public protest meetings were held in Hebden Bridge and, as a result, a voluntary group of enthusiasts formed the action group 'The Friends of the Picture House'. They held their first meeting at the cinema on 16th September 1996 and their spokesperson, Susan Burns, said that they would campaign vigorously to secure the cinema's long-term future.

Local butcher and Member of Parliament, Sir Donald Thompson, a passionate supporter of local interests who regularly took local brass bands to play on the terrace of the House of Commons, put forward the idea of getting together a group of local business people to buy and run the loss-making cinema. He explained that they would need to obtain financial help from the National Lottery to make it work.

Susan Burns, speaking for the Friends of the Picture House, rejected the idea saying that there were examples in the country where cinemas were run by community trusts in partnership with the Council. She was of the opinion that the future of Hebden Bridge Cinema lay with that kind of partnership. She was supported in this by representatives of the Hebden Bridge Light Opera Society.

The Friends of the Picture House energetically lobbied Council meetings until the development plans were eventually dropped, and the Council was persuaded that the cinema should be retained as a local community amenity. The 'Friends' was disbanded as their job at this point was done.

Calderdale Council decided to transfer the control of the cinema from the Council's Halls and Entertainments Committee to Museums and Arts, where improvements could be closely managed by Arts Development Officer, Fi Godfrey-Faussett and her team. Also around this time, Maurice Robson retired from service at the Picture House.

Let's pause here to share the memories of local man, Graham Cobham, whose family were closely involved with the cinema during some of these challenging times.

Graham Cobham and his brother, Michael, remember their parents working at the Picture House from around the early 1960's to the mid 1970's.

"My Dad, Tom Cobham, worked as an engineer in Mytholmroyd during the day and then came to work at the cinema in the evenings. He was a very technical man, not a great film buff, but he was passionate about the Picture House. His main role was as projectionist but he also used to programme the films and take care of the publicity for them too. He was a great reader and he used to read the press to find out which films were being released and which would be popular, so that he could book them to screen at the cinema.

My Mum, Dora Cobham, was employed at Burnley Road School in Mytholmroyd during the day, and then started work at the Picture House for the evening screenings. She would sell tickets, work in the kiosk and then go into the auditorium to work as an usherette and sell ice-creams from her tray during the interval. Dora loved watching films with stars such as Omar Sharif. She saw 'Dr Zhivago' several times at work but always in bits!

Lloyd Brearley was the Picture House Manager at that time and he used to give my parents a lift home after work each night. I remember hearing them arrive home at about 11.30pm and Lloyd would always say "I'll see you anon, Tom". Then I knew they were home. Lloyd Brearley was tall and thin. He worked his staff hard but he was a nice man, usually jovial. He always drove big cars, like Zephyrs.

I used to go to the matinees and, if the film broke, everyone would stamp their feet. I would feel defensive and want to say "My Dad's doing his best!" I would sometimes take my girlfriend to the cinema and my Mum would shine a torch at us if we got up to anything on the back row!

The Picture House was run by a very small team and they all had to work hard to keep it going.

My brother, Michael, and I used to help out at the cinema too. I used to go around and light the gas lights in the auditorium before the screenings and I did my stint selling ice-creams and cleaning up too!

I would also sit up in the projection box with my Dad and watch for the spot to appear in the right hand top corner of the picture to indicate that the reel needed to be changed. The spot was only shown for eight seconds and I had to let my Dad know to switch to the next reel.

Michael used to help in the projection room too. There was a separate winding room and we had to check the film before it was shown, mend any breaks and wind it on. After the screening, the film had to be wound back ready for the next showing.

At the end of every screening we had to close down the film, switch on the footlights and play 'God Save The Queen'. Most people had already left before we got through 'God Save The Queen'!

74

In about 1967, we were doing 'The History of Mr Polly' as our book at school. I got my Dad to screen the film of it at the Picture House, so that me and my friends could watch it. My Dad thought that it was a great idea and, over the next few years, he would find out which book the school was studying and try to book the film at the Picture House for the children to watch.

Lloyd introduced 'Midnight Movies' to try to generate more income for the cinema around the early '70's. These would start at 11.30pm, and were usually 'Hammer Horror' films. They were well-attended and there were usually a few drunks there!

Once, Lloyd showed a 16mm film of 'Mrs Miniver' from a small projector in the auditorium. He got into trouble with the authorities but they let him off as the cinema was just a small private business.

My parents gave many years of loyal service to the Picture House and they were part of the small team who helped to keep it working through some difficult years."

4.14 Tom and Dora Cobham, photograph courtesy of the Cobham family

5. Turn of the Tide

"It struck me that the movies had spent more than half a century saying, 'They lived happily ever after,' and the following quarter-century warning that they'll be lucky to make it through the weekend. Possibly now we are entering a third era in which the movies will be sounding a note of cautious optimism: You know it just might work."
Nora Ephron (8)

As we enter the late 1990's and early 2000's with our story, we find Hebden Bridge developing into a thriving, innovative, vibrant town, priding itself on its resilience, diversity and spirit. At Hebden Bridge Cinema, the closer 'hands-on' management style was also beginning to show results.

Special film events were introduced in 1997 to tempt audiences back into the cinema. For example, there was a very successful Halloween evening special where film-goers dressed as vampires or waved bulbs of garlic to claim their discounted cocktails!

5.1 Halloween event at the Picture House, 1997, Picture House Archives

5.2 Halloween event at the Picture House, 1997, Picture House Archives

On another evening, Kenneth Branagh's brilliant adaptation of Shakespeare's 'Hamlet' was screened, whilst Danish pastries and hot drinks were served. These special events were attended by large and appreciative audiences.

During the Christmas holiday in 1997, Frank Capra's 1946 popular heart-warming film 'It's A Wonderful Life' was screened. Little did the cinema staff at the time realise that this would kick-start a Hebden Bridge tradition. Every year this film is screened to a packed house on Christmas Eve to get the town into the festive spirit!

5.3 It's A Wonderful Life, 1946, 50th Anniversary poster, Public Domain

In Britain generally, things were looking up for cinema and the film industry. The incoming Blair government of 1997 prioritised the provision of more support for film-makers. They set up the U.K. Film Council, a non-departmental public body, created to support British film-making. There was also a steady growth in cinema audiences across the country during this period. We must realise, however, that some of this increased interest in cinema-going was due to the popularity of the multiplexes, so times were still challenging for small independent cinemas.

On 8th March 1998, Hebden Bridge Cinema closed for a major refurbishment of the foyer and entrance. On the last evening before the closure a sell-out audience watched the popular film 'Brassed Off'. This is a drama based around a colliery brass band at the time of the miners' strikes and pit closures. Grimethorpe Colliery Band provided the music for the film and some of the scenes were filmed at the Piece Hall in Halifax. The audience was entertained by the Hebden Bridge Junior Band whilst Crown Fisheries sold pies and mushy peas.

The cinema was closed for three weeks for the refurbishment. The original tiles framing the entrance were stripped of layers of red paint and restored while the foyer, with its new kiosk, was decorated in subtle 1920's shades of green, blue and brown. By popular demand, the cinema reverted to its original name. The board which read 'HEBDEN BRIDGE CINEMA' was replaced by a new illuminated 'HEBDEN BRIDGE PICTURE HOUSE' sign. The Picture House was the Picture House once more!

The cinema re-opened on Saturday 28th March 1998, with plans to become the best small cinema in the country. Fi Godfrey-Faussett remarked:

"There's a lot we haven't got but we have got atmosphere, that feel good feeling as you walk up the steps! We can't rival a multiplex but we can offer a more personal style - from a family focus to challenge and choice for serious film fans."

The re-opening took the form of a gala period event with the screening of the blockbuster film 'Titanic'. Music for the evening was provided by the 'Duchy Palm Court Trio' and film-goers were able to enjoy canapés and 'iceberg' cocktails. They were also invited to enter into the mood of the event by wearing period costume.

5.4 Palm Court Trio, 1998, Hebden Bridge Times

In 1998, a major change was made to the way films were booked for screening by the Picture House. Bill Lawrence, with his team at Pictureville Cinema, an arts cinema in Bradford, part of the National Museum of Photography, Film & Television (now the National Media Museum), assumed responsibility for booking films into the Picture House. He became a member of the cinema's promotion team and worked closely with Fi Godfrey-Faussett. This resulted in the Picture House being able to secure films much sooner after their release than previously. It also meant that the management could obtain films which fitted into particular themed events and programmes at the cinema.

Over the next couple of years, the cinema management team developed a broad, innovative and diverse programming policy. Family matinees, arthouse films, foreign language films, LGBT interest, as well as main stream blockbusters and classics found their place in the programme.

A Saturday 'Kids' Club' for youngsters aged four to ten was also started around this time. The aim of this twice monthly club was to encourage the children to be creative with art and craft activities as well as having the opportunity to enjoy a film.

All of these special film events, gala nights, family matinees, children's clubs and the broad-based film programming policy helped the Picture House to appeal to as many people in the area as possible and to re-establish the cinema's place as a centre of the local community.

Irfan Ajeeb, of the National Museum of Photography, Film and Television (now the National Media Museum) in Bradford, who scheduled films for the Picture House said:

"Hebden Bridge's cinema has such a reputation now that major studios such as '20th Century Fox' are very happy to offer their big budget movies close to release date."

The staff structure at the Picture House was also under scrutiny during this period of regrouping and improvement. There had been no on-site manager at the cinema since 1993 and the front of house staff were all on casual temporary contracts. The Council team decided that a strong core staff was needed to ensure the future smooth, efficient running of the Picture House. An on-site manager was appointed and from then onwards most of the staff were employed on permanent contracts.

A loyalty scheme for cinema-users was introduced. This was called 'Picture This' and is still popular with regular visitors today.

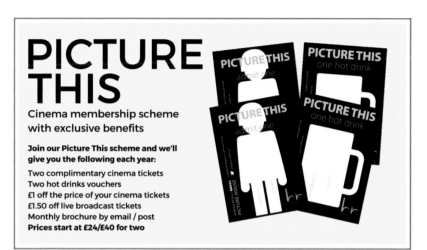

PICTURE THIS

Cinema membership scheme
with exclusive benefits

Join our Picture This scheme and we'll
give you the following each year:

Two complimentary cinema tickets
Two hot drinks vouchers
£1 off the price of your cinema tickets
£1.50 off live broadcast tickets
Monthly brochure by email / post
Prices start at £24/£40 for two

5.5 'Picture This' membership, Courtesy of the Picture House

An interesting article appeared in the local paper around this time, reporting that two national conferences, one in London and one in Nottingham, highlighted Hebden Bridge Picture House as an example of 'best practice in local cinema'. A spokesman from the British Film Institute described it as 'a role model for the future'.

Although the cinema's performance was improving, Calderdale Council was still very concerned about the amount of financial support it required. This, unfortunately, resulted in yet another re-development plan being put forward in July 1999.

The plan involved part of the centre of Hebden Bridge, in particular the Picture House site and the area between that and the canal marina. The idea was to build a much smaller cinema and a 'Canal Interpretation Centre' to create an area of interest for visitors to the town. The intention was to show how the canal had developed, and how technology was used to improve the environment.

This plan, involving the demolition of the Picture House, was accepted by a meeting of Calderdale Council. Three of the founding members of the 'Friends of the Picture

House' action group, Lee Comer, Liz North, and Richard Peters were quoted as saying:

"When we first launched the 'Friends' in 1996, the Council was keen to consult us and we worked with them to revitalise the cinema. Now it appears that decisions regarding the future of the Picture House are being made without consultation with the local community. The present threat to the cinema appears to be an almost repeat of that of three years ago when the 'Friends of the Picture House' worked to persuade the Council to drop their re-development plans for the cinema. The 'Friends' action group should be re-formed to ensure that the local support for the cinema is recognised by the Council."

Immediately, a campaign to save the cinema was launched by Councillor Stewart Brown who considered the demolition of the cinema to be an act of municipal vandalism. Councillor Brown, as Chairman of Calderdale's Rural Challenge Partnership, urged Calderdale Council to reconsider its decision. He said:

"It's not like other cinemas. There's just so much love attached to it, especially for older people who have used the cinema for much of their lives."

Soon afterwards, another meeting of the Council put the plan on hold - but only on the casting vote of the Chairman. At a subsequent meeting, the Council excluded the Picture House from the plans because it had become clear that the people of Hebden Bridge did not want the cinema to be included in the proposed development.

Councillor Brown had been a stalwart supporter of the Picture House over the years, championing the cinema when times were hard. In fact, he and former Mayor of Hebden Bridge, Les Siddall, were convinced that the cinema would not be safe from demolition until it was listed. Backed by a petition signed by over five thousand people, they wrote to the Department of Culture, Media and Sport asking them to 'spot list' the building. Those in favour of the listing argued that it would provide extra bureaucratic process which would hinder any proposed development of the site. Of course, the other side of the debate would contend that once a building is listed, it is more complicated and time-consuming to arrange any modernisation or refurbishment. Also, a listing would not necessarily protect the interior of the building or its function as a cinema. Clearly, however, the overwhelming desire of the local community was to try to protect the cinema. The listing was ratified in December 1999. It is Grade II listed as a building of special historical and architectural interest. The listing report describes the cinema as follows:

"Cinema and flanking shops. 1919-21, with minor late C20 alterations. Brick with coursed rubble and ashlar facade, plus slate roofs. Street front has recessed central section reached up flight of 11 steps, with single giant Doric columns in antis with and pilasters supporting deep entablature. This entrance has original glazed tiles, glazed doors with contemporary frames, and to left original canted wooden box office with original glazing. Centre topped with entablature which continues either side over projecting side wings with rusticated quoins at the corners. Each side wing has a shop on each side with contemporary shopfronts, each with a recessed central doorway, topped with row of overlights and fascia boards. Above each section has 3 windows the central one with ashlar surround and pediment. The whole facade topped by deep plain parapet, the recessed central section has stepped centre originally topped by a flagpole. INTERIOR has original foyer with original panelling and coved and decorated plaster ceiling and doors. Original staircase to left leads to balcony above with doorways and doorcases. Auditorium retains most of its original Classical style decoration. Walls decorated with panels and pilaster strips between with decorative tops. Curved ceiling has simple panel decoration. Procenium has panelled sides and moulded frame which has been removed on lower sections. In front is orchestra pit.

Curved balcony has panelled facade. Seats replaced with thirties seating from another cinema."(9)

In 2000, The Calder Valley was used as a back-drop for filming once again, this time, a short film based on a poem 'The Tyre', by Simon Armitage. The film starred Christopher Eccleston and was shot around Heptonstall. It used local people as extras and also featured children from The Ridings School in Halifax. In it, Christopher Eccleston plays a disgruntled sales rep. who has to stop to change a flat tyre on his car. The spare tyre runs away from him down a steep hill. As he gives chase, he is suddenly able to reconnect with memories of forgotten childhood magic, helping to release him from his frustrations. A special screening of the film was held at Hebden Bridge Picture House on December 12th, 2000.

5.6 Christopher Eccleston in 'The Tyre', 2000, Copyright FilmFour

In 2001, the Picture House celebrated eighty years of film screening with a festival of silent movies, themed evenings and community activities. Films chosen to mark the anniversary on July 11th were 'Never Weaken', starring Harold Lloyd, and Buster Keaton's 'Steamboat Bill'. Live accompanying music was provided by 'The Harmonie Band' with pupils from Calder High and Todmorden High School.

Anna Smith, Picture House Manager at the time said:
"We're hoping that as many people as possible will dress in 1920's gear for the occasion".

The event was a great success and even the Mayor, Councillor Michelle Hanley-Foster, got into the spirit of the evening by dressing in 1920's garb!

5.7 'Steamboat Bill' opening screenshot, 1928, Public Domain

5.8 'Never Weaken' publicity poster 1921, Public Domain

On July 12th, the old Hebden Bridge favourite, the 1949 romantic comedy 'A Boy, A Girl and a Bike' starring Honor Blackman and Diana Dors, was screened. There was also a showing of archival film of Hebden Bridge's 1920's carnival. The celebration concluded with a screening of 'Captain Correlli's Mandolin'. The success of this event showed once again that there was huge community support for the cinema and that it remained at the heart of Hebden Bridge life.

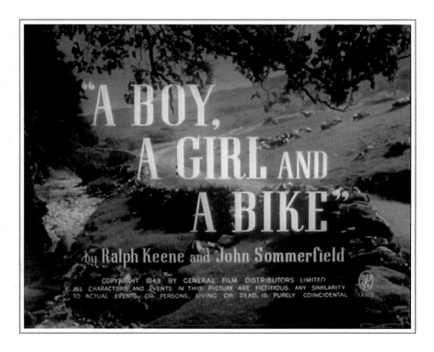

5.9 'A Boy, A Girl And a Bike' opening screenshot, 1949, Copyright Gainsborough Pictures

Around the time of the eightieth anniversary celebrations, Emily Fussell took over as manager of the Picture House. She continued the challenging work of maintaining the appeal of the cinema to all sections of the community. One project she undertook was to ask local cinema-goers to vote for their top three favourite films of all time, with a view to showing the most popular choices at Christmas-time. At the time, Emily said:

"It's a bit of fun and it is all about getting to know what our punters like".

Over the next few years, the Picture House did manage to maintain its position in Hebden Bridge as a popular entertainment venue, meeting place and treasured landmark at the centre of the community - steering its own course through a competitive marketplace. It did this by screening a much more eclectic selection of films than the multiplexes, hosting live events, providing a warm, intimate atmosphere and connecting with the local townspeople. In 2004, newly appointed manager, Jen Skinner, was quoted as saying:

"You have to have a programme that is as varied as possible. We do have a very varied and mixed audience so you have to make sure all tastes are covered."

Jen had been Duty Manager at the Picture House for three years prior to accepting the role of Manager so she was already familiar with her audience!

Two popular live events that year were 'An Evening With Gervaise Phinn' and a lively debate on subjects ranging from politics to women in Shakespeare, hosted by Germaine Greer.

In 2005, the Picture House reported that ticket sales for the year had risen by more than three thousand compared to the previous year.

On the evening of Wednesday 24th September 2008, Hebden Bridge Local History Group opened their season with a presentation entitled 'Hebden Royd at the Movies, Celebrating Eighty Eight Years of 'Callywood''. This event was held at the Picture House and celebrated films shot in the local area during the eighty eight years since 1920. It featured extracts from feature films, films of local events, as well as talks and comments by celebrities. It was well-attended and proved to be very popular.

The following year, they hosted a similar event, again at the Picture House, which also featured some stills from the 1920 film 'Helen of Four Gates'. This was the first known public screening of any part of this film since the 1920's.

This film, made in 1920, was directed by Cecil Hepworth. A pioneer of early motion pictures, he was too ambitious in the expansion of his studio, over-reached himself financially and was declared bankrupt in 1924. His original negatives and prints were seized and melted down for the value of the silver nitrate in the film strips. It was assumed that 'Helen of Four Gates' had been lost in this way. However, research conducted by Chris Lynch in 2007 indicated that there was an original surviving print of the movie in the archives of La Cinémathèque Québécoise in Montreal, and another 16mm version in the George Eastman House Museum in New York. After years of effort and detective work, local film-maker, Nick Wilding, managed to locate the print in Canada and worked with the British Film Institute to re-patriate the print to Britain.

5.10 Alma Taylor in 'Helen of Four Gates", 1920, Copyright Hepworth

In 2010, as part of the celebrations to mark the five hundredth anniversary of the re-building of Hebden Bridge's packhorse bridge, 'Helen of Four Gates' was screened in its entirety for the first time in ninety years. It was screened at the Picture House to a packed audience.

'Helen of Four Gates' was based on a novel by former mill girl, Ethel Carnie Holdsworth, who lived in Heptonstall in the 1920's. Hepworth used the Pennine moors around Heptonstall and Hebden Bridge for the film's location and local people appeared as extras. Actress Alma Taylor starred in the dual role of mother and daughter.

Very sadly, on 11th June 2009, the Picture House lost a loyal and hardworking member of staff. Roger Bogg worked as projectionist at the Picture House for more than forty years. He passed away at the cinema preparing for the next screening and doing the job that he loved. He had often said that he was doing the best job in the world.

Roger's life of dedication to the cinema was celebrated with screenings of a selection of his favourite films. Included was the short film 'The Projectionist', shot at the Picture House in 2007, and 'Better Than Sex', another beautiful short film that featured Roger's thoughts on projection and the magic of cinema. The Picture House manager at the time, Jonny Courtney said:

"These films are a celebration of Roger's life and times at the Picture House. We have chosen films that we are sure would have pleased him immensely."

The Halifax Courier published a report which informed readers that profits from the memorial screenings would be re-invested in the cinema and, in particular, a new screen would be purchased.

5.11 Roger Bogg, photograph courtesy of Martin Parr © Martin Parr / Magnum Photos

Lorraine Mitchell began work at The Picture House in 1987 and, as Duty Manager, she has been able to witness many challenges and changes. She also has fond memories of Roger Bogg. Her comments (below) provide us with an eye-witness account of these turbulent times:

"In the late eighties and early nineties the cinema was very different to how it is now. We showed what I call 'Crash, Bang, Wallop' films a lot of the time. At weekends, things could get pretty lively! Sometimes, people used to hide bottles of vodka in the cistern of the toilets at the cinema, so they could go in and get a drink during the film. We also had to sit the Todmorden lot on the opposite side of the auditorium to the Hebden lot, as there could be trouble between them at the end of the film.

The balcony was open at every screening, but unaccompanied children were not allowed up there. It didn't stop them though because they used to go into the stalls and then climb the curtains to get up into the balcony!

P.C. Lemon was our local Bobby and he used to pop in most nights for tea and cake. At the weekends, he used to walk up and down the aisles to make sure everyone was behaving. The kids respected him. There was a lady called Barbara, who did the paperwork and sold the tickets.

Things changed a lot when Fi Godfrey-Faussett came along. The 'Crash, Bang, Wallop' films stopped, and she changed the programme a lot, so that the adults started coming back to the cinema. One of the first films we showed after she started was 'Il Postino', which surprised a lot of the regulars! I made the poster for that one, because we didn't have one.

We had a major refurb in 1998. We showed 'Brassed Off' first and the queue of people who wanted to see it went all around the building. I bet we turned away a full house of people that night because we were sold out! We were shut for a few weeks, and when we opened we showed 'Titanic', and we had canapés and a string quartet.

We had lots of special events. For the eightieth anniversary of the Picture House, I remember, the ushers all had to wear black uniforms with white aprons. Then we had Oscars Night with fancy dress and Bond Night with roulette.

It was a fantastic night when we first showed 'Fanny and Elvis', as it was filmed in the town. We had a red carpet, the cinema was decorated in purple and silver, and we all had party poppers.

We also had a kids' club, which was held in the balcony. The kids loved it because it was the only time they were allowed there on their own - it was their time. If it was one of the children's birthdays, they got to go into the projection room, and push the button to start the film, which they loved.

I worked with Roger Bogg for years. He used to call me 'Sweet', which was short for 'Sweet Lorraine', as in the song. Roger could be cantankerous, but we got on well. He was very intelligent with a really wide knowledge - he'd have been good in a pub quiz! He had a full-time job as a builder, and worked at the Picture House part-time. He only claimed twelve hours a week on his time-sheet, but he was here six days a week, and every weekend, and he did all the backstage jobs as well as being the projectionist - it was his life. I remember once, he fell off a ladder changing a light bulb here. We had to take him to A&E, but he was still back at work on time for the next film.

When the film broke, he always mended it, and managed to restart it at exactly the point where it had stopped. Once, he turned the projector by hand for an entire film, when he couldn't get it working. He came out of the projection room, red and dripping with sweat! When we told the audience what he'd done, they all applauded him. He also got applause when we showed 'Cinema Paradiso'. The film was in such a bad condition that it would hardly play. Roger nursed that film through from beginning to end and managed to show the whole film.

They played the music from 'Cinema Paradiso' at Roger's funeral - the place was packed. I have never known *anyone as dedicated as him, he was the continuity at the Picture House, and it took a long time to settle after he died."*

6. Jewel in the Crown

"The art I make is similar to film – my paintings are essentially freeze frames from movies that are playing in my head. I think it's pretty clear that film is the pre-eminent art form of our age. If Michaelangelo or Leonardo Da Vinci were alive today they'd be making 'Avatar', not painting a chapel. Film is incredibly democratic and accessible, it's probably the best option if you actually want to change the world, not just re-decorate it."
Banksy (10)

As we begin this chapter we find Hebden Bridge Picture House, a grand old lady of nearly ninety, setting a course for her journey through the twenty first century. The cinema, treasured by the people of Hebden Bridge, is very much a part of the identity of the town.

6.1 Hebden Bridge Picture House, 2006, Copyright Nigel Homer and licensed for reuse under this Creative Commons Licence - http://www.geograph.org.uk/photo/ 142512

6.2 Picture House steps, 2008, Copyright Robert Wade and licensed for reuse under this Creative Commons Licence - http://www.geograph.org.uk/photo/708923

On 4th March 2011, four months before the ninetieth anniversary of the cinema opening, a packed public meeting at Riverside School debated whether Hebden Royd Town Council should take control of the cinema in order to ensure its survival.

A Hebden Royd Town Council representative told the meeting that discussions were beginning with Calderdale Council with the object of bringing the building into the Town Council's control. Grant funding of the cinema had ceased under Calderdale's administration, and it was suggested that the transfer should be done as a matter of urgency because the long term survival of the cinema could not be guaranteed by the short-of-cash Calderdale Council.

On 1st December 2011, Hebden Royd Town Council together with Hebden Bridge Community Association made an asset transfer proposal to Calderdale Council for the cinema. This was accepted, and Hebden Royd Town Council took over the Picture House on a one hundred and twenty five year lease on 1st April 2012 with a view to maintaining it as a valued amenity.

6.3 Public meeting, 2011, photograph courtesy of Chris Ratcliffe

A successful asset transfer had taken place the previous year, when the Hebden Bridge Community Association took control of Hebden Bridge Town Hall. As in the case of the Town Hall, the aim of this transfer was to harness local energy and creativity to strengthen the position of the Picture House. A stated objective was the production of a ten-year strategic plan which would seek to extend the facilities and the use made of the building.

Councillor Susan Press, Chair of the Town Council's Picture House Committee said:

"It was the old Urban District Council which stepped in during the late 1960's to prevent the cinema from closing, and

it is appropriate that the Town Council now once again will be bringing direct control of the cinema back to Hebden Bridge. This marks a significant move forward in the role which the Town Council is playing in our community life."

6.4 Duncan Watson (Chair of Friends of Picture House committee), Paul Knights (Secretary of Friends of the Picture House committee), Councillor Susan Press (Chair of Picture House committee), Michael Coneys (Friends of the Picture House committee), Rebekah Fozard (Vice-Chair of Friends of the Picture House and future Picture House Manager), Jason Boom (Town Clerk) and Mayor of Hebden Royd Councillor, Scott Trickett, 2012, Hebden Bridge Times

When Hebden Royd Town Council took over the running of the Picture House, it was decided that the Friends of the Picture House group should be re-established to further increase the input of the community into the future of the cinema. The Friends would be set up as a voluntary group to represent all users of the Picture House. This group would be open and free for all to join. A committee would be elected to consider what the Friends wanted from the cinema and how its future could be assured. The first committee was elected in

97

November 2011 at a public meeting which took place at Riverside School in Hebden Bridge.

The inaugural meeting of the re-formed Friends of the Picture House group took place at the Town Hall on 5th December 2011. One of the first issues discussed was how it could assist the Town Council Picture House Management Committee and the cinema management in their efforts to maintain and promote the Picture House as a local amenity.

To this day the Friends of the Picture House continues to operate in this way. It supports the Picture House with fundraising activities, managing donations and practical help (such as decorating, cleaning, voluntary help at fundraising events). It also seeks to represent all cinema users as decisions are made regarding future development. The Friends' elected committee meets regularly to consider what its members want from the Picture House and how they can ensure that the cinema continues to thrive. Two members of the Friends' committee attend the Town Council's Picture House Management Committee meetings to ensure that the views of cinema-goers are also well represented there.

At time of going to press there were 640 members of the Friends of the Picture House. Membership is free and open to anyone who has an interest in seeing the Picture House continue to cater for the diverse interests of its visitors.

A Gala Night was held at the Picture House in April 2012 to celebrate the transfer of control to the Town Council. A packed auditorium enjoyed an evening of entertainment. Former Mayor, Robin Dixon, acted as Master of Ceremonies, and there were speeches from current Mayor of Calderdale, Cllr Nader Fekri, and Mayor of Hebden Royd, Cllr Scott Trickett. Kay Mellor, Director of 'Fanny & Elvis', put in a guest appearance before the film itself was screened.

6.5 Queue for Gala Night, 2012, photograph Jason Boom

6.6 Gala Night, 2012, photograph Jason Boom

6.7 Mayor of Hebden Royd, Cllr Scott Trickett with Kay Mellor, hebdenroyd .org.uk

In the months following the transfer, the Picture House thrived. This was despite an initial set-back in 2012 when it flooded after a period of very wet weather. Prudent development and promotion of the cinema by an enlightened management team resulted in audiences growing considerably. Programming was carefully planned to cater for all tastes, ranging from mainstream Hollywood to art-house and foreign language films.

To ensure that the most modern films could be screened, a digital projection system costing over £50,000 was installed in July 2012. It was paid for by Hebden Royd households who were asked for a one-off £10 average increase in their council tax. Newly-appointed Cinema Manager, Rebekah Fozard, said that without digital projection the cinema would have been forced to close. It could not have competed with other cinemas which did have digital equipment, since many new film releases had digital-only distribution. The 35mm projection system at the Picture House was retained, however, so that classic older films could still be screened.

6.8 Original 1950's 35mm projector, photograph courtesy of Bruce Cutts, After Alice Project

For the benefit of people with hearing difficulties audio headsets offering amplification of the sound were now on hand. For the visually impaired audio description was available on some films. The auditorium already had nine spaces allocated for wheelchair-users.

6.9 Digital projection system installed alongside 1950's projector, Ben Gwilliam, projectionist, at work, photograph courtesy of Bruce Cutts, After Alice Project

In 2012, the Town Council's acceptance of the Picture House as a valuable town asset together with the investment in digital projection equipment proved to be a major turning point in the fortunes of the cinema and the start of its salvation. Jason Boom, Town Clerk of Hebden Royd Town Council, said, in the cinema's first annual report, that while striving for an operating surplus to reinvest in the business, it is not profit-driven. The Picture House operates to serve the whole community and remains available for community use.

6.10 Jason Boom, Town Clerk of Hebden Royd Town Council

The management team led by Cinema Manager, Rebekah Fozard, and backed by the Friends of the Picture House, worked together with the Town Council with significant success. Rebekah's involvement in films goes back to university where she was a projectionist, then Secretary, then President of the St. John's College Film Society. She studied Law and worked as a commercial property solicitor for seven years before moving to Square Chapel Centre for the Arts in 2010, whilst undertaking a Masters Degree in Arts Management. In her post at the Picture House, her management skills were tested to the full as she and Programming and Marketing Officer, Jonny Courtney, guided the fortunes of the cinema.

103

6.11 Rebekah Fozard, Picture House Manager with Hebden Royd Town Council Mayor, Cllr Christine Davenport and Deputy Mayor, Cllr Karl Boggis, - Working whilst cinema staff enjoyed their Christmas meal out! photograph Jason Boom

In addition to being the setting for carefully programmed film screenings, the Picture House continued to be used for events involving people of the local area. The cinema hosted shows for Hebden Bridge Arts Festival and this together with other professional live events, such as high quality music and literature productions, attracted good audiences and also tended to enhance the image of the Picture House as an entertainment venue.

Another exciting venture around this time was the live broadcast of entertainment from venues and theatres around the world, which the Picture House began in 2013, following the installation of a satellite dish and receiver. These programmes were received via satellite and screened at the cinema. This regular live streaming of events continues to be a popular part of the programme shown at the Picture House as well as an important income stream.

A few examples of some of the shows enjoyed by cinema-goers at the Picture House include 'Macbeth' from Manchester International Festival, 'The Audience' and 'War Horse' broadcast from The National Theatre, 'The Nutcracker' ballet from The Royal Opera House, Covent Garden, 'A Winter's Tale' from the Royal Shakespeare Theatre, Stratford-upon-Avon and 'The Railway Children' from the Theatre Royal, York.

Since the transfer of control to Hebden Royd Town Council the cinema management has continued to be on the look-out for ways of promoting film entertainment and attracting fresh clientele. The Halloween Festival on 31st October 2015 was a one day affair which started at two o'clock in the afternoon and finished after midnight. The programme of five horror classics included 'The Wicker Man' as a tribute to Sir Christopher Lee. It marked the beginning of monthly Saturday tea-time showings of 'Surreal Reels', a feast of transgressive screenings celebrating twisted and macabre tales from cinema's finest film-makers. Not to be missed! Other Saturday tea-time screenings to be enjoyed are 'Tea-Time Classics', where favourite iconic old movies are brought back to the big screen, 'Reel Film', where 35mm film is shown on the cinema's original 1950's projector, and 'Friends Presents', where the Friends of the Picture House are able to vote for their favourite films to be screened and host the screenings. To accompany the 'Friends Presents' screenings complimentary food is served by members of the Friends committee. The food is carefully chosen to tie-in with the chosen film. So for instance, cinema-goers attending 'Ferris Bueller's Day Off' were treated to pizza and paczki (polish doughnuts), both representative of Chicago where the film is set. Black bean brownies and cocadas (coconut cookies) were served as a Bolivian flavour to accompany 'Butch Cassidy and the Sundance Kid'.

Favourites, such as the 'Elevenses' screenings on Thursday mornings with its mugs of tea or coffee and biscuits, continued to attract large audiences and newer ideas like 'Parent and Baby' performances were also introduced. It was hoped that, in the long term, these monthly 'Parent and Baby' shows would benefit the local community and also establish a permanent connection between the cinema and families.

Financially, the cinema management could also claim that their methods were successful as operating surpluses showed a steady increase over the years 2012/13 to 2014/15. All seemed to be going well until, on 26th December 2015, disaster struck Hebden Bridge and the Picture House and put all plans on hold. The cinema had to fight for survival once again.

After heavy and persistent rainfall the flood defences around Hebden Bridge proved inadequate and the town was deluged. Most businesses and residences in the centre of town were under several feet of water. Only when the flood subsided and the buildings were accessible again could the extent of the devastation be assessed. At the Picture House flood water up to five or six feet deep had rushed through the cinema, coming from both the canal at the rear and over the eleven steps at the front of the building. The auditorium and the basement boiler room were inundated. The foyer, all of the downstairs seating, and the carpets and curtains were ruined. Only the projection room, the stage, dressing rooms and the balcony seating were high enough not to have been affected.

How forlorn our Picture House looked the following day, the auditorium dimly lit by head-torches and flood-lights as a group consisting of cinema staff, Friends of the Picture House members and other townspeople gathered to miserably survey the wreckage, and begin the shovelling, sweeping, mopping and scrubbing.

6.12 Hebden Bridge town centre (December 2015), Chris Ratcliffe

6.13 New Road flooded, Picture House on left side of road (December 2015), Chris Ratcliffe

A massive clean-up operation was also underway in the rest of Hebden Bridge. The townspeople once again showed their loyalty, resilience and courage, as everyone pulled together to get the town back on its feet. Over the following four days, Picture House staff together with many generous volunteers cleaned the auditorium and foyer area. Then, armed with power tools, they removed the sodden seats in the stalls.

The Picture House was actually closed for only five days, after which film screening resumed using the balcony seats only. There was no heating when it re-opened, as the boiler had not been replaced, so cinema-goers were issued with a cosy red blanket when they bought their ticket!

6.14 Willing volunteers at the Picture House (December 2015), Paul Knights

6.15 Cleaning up the flooded foyer (December 2015), HebWeb

6.16 The 'Not-so-grand Re-opening' New Year's Day 2016, Courtesy of the Picture House

6.17 Loyal cinema goers queue for the first screening after the floods, Paul Knights

6.18 Wrapped up in warm clothes and blankets in the balcony, Paul Knights

During the repairs, the management still did their best to maintain an innovative, broad-ranging programme at the cinema. For example, a documentary, 'Stronger Than Death', about the life of the late Poet Laureate, Ted Hughes, was screened. It focused on the events of his life and the influence of his poetry. After the film a panel which included the film's directors, Richard Curson Smith and Ross Wilson, took over and the audience was involved in a lively question and answer session.

Before new seats were fitted in the auditorium, the opportunity was taken to gain access to the very high ceiling, using a 'cherry-picker', to survey and then repair the plain and ornate plasterwork. The central heating boiler room was relocated to a higher level, out of reach of any future flood, and heating was restored at the end of January. New seats were then fitted in the stalls and the work in the auditorium was completed by Easter. The whole cinema re-opened on Good Friday, 25th March 2016.

Many generous donations were received by the Friends of the Picture House to help with recovery after the floods. For instance, Hebden Bridge Twinning Society received, on behalf of the Picture House, an incredibly generous donation of 2,000 Euros from St Pol-sur-Ternoise Council, Hebden Bridge's twin town in France.

6.19 Volunteers remove the sodden seats from the stalls, Rebekah Fozard

6.20 Auditorium restored to its former glory, Sarah Mason Photography

6.21 Refurbished giltwork in auditorium, Sarah Mason Photography

Flooding is, unfortunately, not a new phenomenon in Hebden Bridge. It is a town situated on the floor of a steep-sided valley which was of benefit when water-mills were essential to local industry. However, heavy, prolonged rain-fall on the moors and hills above the town will, inevitably, result in a rise in water levels and the risk of flooding.

The earliest record of severe flooding was in 1615, when a bridge at Elland was swept away. In November 1767 and February 1768, during the extension of the Upper Calder Navigation, flooding was so severe in the Sowerby Bridge region that work on the canal was stopped until the engineer, James Brindley, had built flood barriers to protect it.

Major floods were recorded in 1837 and 1859, when the whole of the centre of Hebden Bridge was flooded to a depth of several feet. Since then, flooding in the Hebden Bridge area has been recorded regularly and, during the twentieth century, roads and properties have been seriously affected at least fifteen times. In fact, as previously mentioned, the Picture House itself was also flooded in 2012, just after the town Council take-over.

© PHDA - Alice Longstaff Collection

6.23 New Road flooded, 1946, Picture House in the centre of the shot, Alice Longstaff Gallery Collection

A refurbishment of the foyer at the Picture House had been planned for some time and, once the flood repairs in the auditorium were complete, work began on this in May, 2016. The plasterwork cornice was repaired, a new kiosk was installed, and the whole painted in deep red and cream with detail picked out in gold leaf. Red curtains were hung at the windows and a new carpet replaced the old, badly stained one. Funds raised by the Friends of the Picture House, together with donations received, were used to buy a pair of chandeliers and wall-lights, a new external film-times board, chairs for carers accompanying wheelchair users, and the refurbishment of an old clock. Years ago, this brass clock used to hang in the auditorium to the left of the screen for the convenience of those patrons needing to catch trams or buses. It had been taken down and left unused for many years in a storage space at the cinema. Projectionist, Graham Tottles, had carefully made sure that it was safe during this time, and continually lobbied for its restoration. Thanks to some remedial work by local specialist, Jonathan Cope, it was returned to its former glory and hung in pride of place above the kiosk in the foyer. Some of the funds used to refurbish this clock also came from Julia Turpin, whose mother, Brenda Turpin, was a regular visitor to The Picture House.

Let's watch the transformation in this series of pictures:

6.24 The foyer pre-refurbishment, early 2016, Roland Higham

6.25 Katharina Heu hard at work, making new sections to match existing cornice, Rebekah Fozard

6.26 Installation of the new kiosk begins, made by 'Wood & Wire', a Hebden Bridge business, Rebekah Fozard

6.27 Kiosk refurbishment complete, Sarah Mason Photography

6.28 Trams long gone, but the clock is restored, Paul Knights

6.29 View towards auditorium, Sarah Mason Photography

6.30 (left) Chandeliers in place, Paul Knights

6.31 (above) Detail of plasterwork, Sarah Mason Photography

118

As finishing touches were being added to the repairs and refurbishments, projectionist Graham Tottles happened upon a very battered but recognisable section of stained glass in the backstage area. It was promptly identified as coming from the 1920's ticket booth on the outside of the building. During a previous refurbishment the stained glass had been removed and replaced with plain panes. Local stained glass specialist, Karl Percival, stepped up and offered to restore the window to its former glory. The result of this work became a truly splendid finishing touch to this lovely building.

6.32 Karl Percival with the restored stained glass window, Rebekah Fozard

Thus, in 2016, the Picture House, excluding the backstage and balcony areas, was completely re-decorated and refurbished. The result is a building and cinema truly worth treasuring: smart paintwork, plush curtains and carpets, gleaming gilt plasterwork, and the same loyal, hardworking

119

team striving to bring a vibrant, eclectic programme of films and events to the people of Hebden Bridge.

6.33 Picture House staff and members of Friends of the Picture House, three minutes to re-opening of the foyer on 3rd June 2016, Rebekah Fozard

Despite its facelift, however, a testing time still lay ahead for the cinema. The Picture House suffered a severe loss of income due to the flooding, which had occurred at the time of the year when audience attendance, and therefore revenue, was normally at its highest. Months after the flood, audience attendance was still well below that recorded in previous years. Indeed, trade in the whole of the town remained slow well into the summer of 2016 and beyond, as the townspeople repaired and resurrected their homes and businesses after the flood damage.

It was calculated in 2012 that, because of high overheads and a legacy of under-investment in the building's fabric and technology, an average of around eighty people attending each screening would be required to cover yearly running costs at the cinema. Worryingly, by early May 2016, the average attendance per screening was still only in the forties. This would not generate sufficient income to keep the cinema open if it continued, as, since April 2012, the cinema had been operated without regular grant funding or subsidy. It was clear that, unless there was a radical improvement in audience attendances during the months that followed, there would be a cash flow problem before the end of the year.

A large scale promotion campaign was instituted by the Picture House management and aided by the Friends of the Picture House. Loyalty schemes were introduced for cinema-goers, programmes and leaflets highlighting the situation were distributed around the town and great attention was paid to maximising publicity. The management team, the Town Council and the Friends of the Picture House were working hard to get the business back on track. Slowly, progress was perceptible. After many leaflets were distributed and local media coverage was sought, audience numbers began to pick up. The Picture House appeared to be on the road to recovery.

Thus we leave the story so far of Hebden Bridge Picture House as thoughts begin to turn towards the centenary of this grand building. Challenges, no doubt, still lie ahead but the Picture House team, the Council and the townspeople seem ready and willing to stand shoulder to shoulder to defend and champion this jewel in the crown of the community.

6.34 Hebden Bridge Picture House, Sarah Mason Photography

6.35 Hebden Bridge Picture House 2016, photograph taken by Raphael Pavel, http://www.raphaeloo.com/

6.36 Lorna Dodd at work in the Picture House, 2016, photograph taken by Raphael Pavel, http://www.raphaeloo.com/

6.37 Hebden Bridge Picture House, 2016, photograph taken by Raphael Pavel, http://www.raphaeloo.com/

Afterword - Musings from the Manager

The enjoyment I gained from reading and re-reading this wonderful book, learning so much I didn't know (and could not have known) about the cinema's first 105 years in operation and 95 years in this building, matches the enjoyment I have gained from managing the Picture House since November 2012.

I often wonder how others in my position in times past, such as Maurice Robson or Lloyd Brearley or the many others whose names are now long forgotten, felt when audience figures inexplicably dropped one month, or water poured in down the side of auditorium walls during a film, or a print failed to arrive in time for the screening or new technology came along and the costs of implementing it had to be found. Did these folk, so passionately tied up in the enterprise of cinematic entertainment as I am, muse about the future of the institution? Did they imagine that one day the same Manager's office would host discussions about how to fittingly celebrate the cinema's centenary, now just a few short years away? Probably not, because, like me, they were more than fully occupied in the never ending circus of ensuring the reels kept turning, and the crowds kept turning up.

Managing the Picture House is without a doubt the best job role I have held, but it is so much more than just a job for me. My cinema roots stem back to my university days when I projected and then programmed 35mm films for the college film society, finally presiding over it. Half the size of the cinema here, and only operational part time, we managed to screen around 16 new release titles per term, with a Pearl and Dean advertising contract (and iconic music!), often to full houses. Ever since then I have been hooked on the magic of cinema: the shared experience of sitting in the dark with dozens of strangers, fully absorbed in the stories and lives unfolding on the big screen, oblivious to anything else for a brief time, a beautiful hiatus to reality.

My time as Manager has been both an exciting and challenging time. The building had a legacy of underinvestment when taken over by Hebden Royd Town Council in April 2012 which we have needed to remedy, and continue to grapple with, whilst working to ensure the business delivers both the funds to do so and, importantly, what the audiences require. The floods of 2015 were, we believe, the worst the building has faced in its century of existence and, in addition to taking six months to refurbish downstairs fully, the extent of the water damage on the building's infrastructure is still being understood. The fabric of the building must not be allowed to become a time-consuming distraction however: as a team we have to continue to ensure that the cinema maintains its relevance in an age of instant digital access and home cinema experience, offering something intangibly 'more' than home streaming of digital content does.

The cinema industry faces many challenges in the years ahead which are only multiplied for independent 'second run' single screen cinemas such as ours. The most notable is the 'day and date' (simultaneous) release of a title across all platforms (multiplex, streaming and DVD/BluRay) which many studios / distributors are favouring now. Frustratingly for us, only able to book a title after the multiplexes (and 'home cinema' fans) have had access to it for 3 or 4 or 5 weeks, our exclusivity of content often comes from being the only cinema within a significant radius to screen contemporary foreign language films, indie studio small budget releases, documentary titles, art house content and retrospective (classic) films.

Whilst recovery from the December 2015 flooding has been incredibly consuming for all involved and the continual need to update technology, improve systems and refurbish the building can divert much energy, the strains of the role have been offset by my joy and immense pride in working in such a beautiful space, in leading a fantastic team of dedicated staff and in working alongside enthusiastic supporters in the guise of the Friends of the Picture House. That our programme goes

125

from strength to strength with the addition of the live satellite broadcast of theatre, ballet, opera, documentaries, music and comedy whilst now including themed mini film festivals and four regular strands of retro films is another source of passion for me. My time as Manager is just the latest chapter in the continuing story of a much treasured cinema that refuses to stand still or to give up. Moving with the times, whatever that comes to mean in the decades ahead, will be the only way to keep cinema relevant to changing audiences and to keep a wonderful building like this one in the heart of small communities such as ours.

People often ask me what they can do specifically or what can be done generally to support the Picture House, and the answer is the same as for the many independent cinemas and theatres up and down the country: give the Picture House your custom. It's that simple, effectively a 'use it or lose it' equation. Without grant funding or any regular financial support we simply need those who love cinema to 'shop local', even if it sometimes means waiting a few weeks to see a film. You could join our Picture This loyalty membership scheme for free tickets and discounts off every visit. Beyond this, join the Friends of the Picture House scheme for free to stay involved or actively offer your support as a volunteer Friends committee member, helping to fundraise or profile raise. Hebden Bridge Picture House is incredibly fortunate to have such a strong and enthusiastic Friends group, which re-formed to oversee the asset transfer of the cinema in 2011-12 and has been practically and financially supportive of the management and staff of the cinema ever since, and never more so than in the aftermath of the Boxing Day floods of 2015.

On this note, I give my heartfelt thanks to Kate Higham and Ray Barnes of the Friends of the Picture House for working so tirelessly in their research, interviews, fact-checking and cross-referencing to produce this incredibly approachable and warm hearted tribute to the Hebden Bridge Picture House. That the book concludes with a brief insight into the fate of other local cinemas of the golden age is a further reminder of how lucky we in the Upper Calder Valley are to have such a gem on our doorstep.

I hope that, if you are not already a regular visitor of our beautiful and homely cinema, after reading this wonderful biography of the place, you will want to become a cinema regular and perhaps even consider becoming its Friend? Hebden Bridge Picture House would be lost without its friends.

Rebekah Fozard,
Picture House Manager
September 2016

References

1. U.K. Cinema Association. 2015. *U.K. cinema admissions and box office.* [On-line]. [accessed June 2016]. Available from: http:// www.cinemauk.org.uk/the-industry/facts-and-figures/uk-cinema-admissions-and-box-office/annual-admissions/.

2. Woolf,V. 1926. The Movies and Reality. *The New Republic.* 4th August.

3. Hebden Bridge Local History Society. Archive Catalogue. Birchcliffe Centre, Hebden Bridge. OM32/M

4. Berger, J. 1991. Keeping a Rendezvous. University of California: Pantheon Books.

5. National Council of Public Morals. Cinema Commission of Inquiry. 1917. The cinema; its present position and future possibilities. London: Williams & Norgate.

6. Bergman, I. 1988. The Magic Lantern. New York: Viking.

7. Pettigrew, D. 2003. I'm a Born Liar: A Fellini Lexicon. New York: Harry N. Abrams, Inc.

8. Ephron, N. 1989. Interview regarding the screenplay for 'When Harry Met Sally'. Los Angeles Times. 27th July.

9. Historic England. 1999. Hebden Bridge Picture House and Attached Flanking Shops, List Entry Summary. [On-line]. [accessed September 2016]. Available from: *https:// historicengland.org.uk/listing/the-list/list-entry/1379945.*

10. Schnack, A J. 2010. All These Wonderful Things. [Online]. [accessed June 2016]. Available from *http:// edendale.typepad.com/weblog/2010/12/banksy-yes-banksy-on-thierry-exit-skepticism-documentary-filmmaking-as-punk.html*

11. Dexter, W. 1925. The England of Dickens. London: Cecil Palmer.

12. Report on opening of Grand Theatre in Halifax. 1889. The ERA. 10th August.

13. Carnie Holdsworth, E. 1909. Our Right to Play. The Woman Worker. 14th April

APPENDIX 1

Historic Cinemas in the Calder Valley

Regal Cinema, Burnley Road, Bacup
(Closed)

Bacup Public Hall, built in 1878, began screening films in September 1910, when it became known as the Gem Cinema. By 1916, it had, however, been renamed The Kozy Picture House.

In 1931, it was demolished and the New Regal Super Cinema was built nearby. This cinema was constructed of stone. It had a white facade with a row of circular shields spelling out the word 'R.E.G.A.L.' Its Art Deco interior side walls were painted with scenic views, and it seated 960 people in the stalls and balcony.

It was taken over by the Star Cinema chain in the late 1950's but sadly closed as a cinema in the late 1960's. It was converted into the New Embassy Bingo Club but was later renamed Roxy Bingo Club. The shields along the front were changed to read 'B.I.N.G.O.' The bingo club closed in 2005 and, to date, it has not been developed and is in a rather dilapidated state.

St. John's Church and War Memorial, Bacup.

[1] *Kozy Cinema, Bacup, Copyright Mike Blakemore and licensed for reuse under this Creative Commons Licence - http://cinematreasures.org/theaters/38907/photos/46660*

[2] Regal Cinema, Bacup, Copyright Mike Blakemore and licensed for reuse under this Creative Commons (Attribution) License, http://cinematreasures.org/theaters/3348/ photos/116823

[3] Regal Cinema, Bacup 2016, Kate Higham

Royal Court Theatre, Rochdale Road, Bacup

In 1886, the Henrietta Street Iron Foundry in Bacup suffered a fire. The building was gutted and had to be abandoned. The surviving exterior walls were used in the building of The Court Theatre, which opened in 1893.

The theatre had two circles supported on cast iron columns. It seated 1,200 people. The upper circle was removed, however, in 1948 when it was thought to be unsafe.

In 1911, The Court Theatre became the Art Picture Palace, although it still staged variety shows until 1930 when the 'talkies' arrived and films became more popular.

It is an unusual building in that it is built on a slope. The facade is only one storey high, but the auditorium descends down the slope.

The cinema closed in the early 1960's to become a bingo hall. In 1968, it was acquired by the Bacup Amateur Operatic and Dramatic Society, and was renamed The Royal Court Theatre. In addition to film screenings live shows are performed.

The theatre is reputed to be haunted and, in addition to strange noises and equipment being thrown about, several apparitions regularly appear! Kitty, an usherette, who used to work at the cinema, and an elderly lady, dressed in black, (called Norah by the cinema staff) have reportedly been seen in the auditorium.

[4] Royal Court Theatre, Bacup 2016, Kate Higham

Gem Theatre, Cornholme
(Demolished)

This cinema, situated in Cornholme, seated 400 people. It closed in 1958 and was subsequently demolished. Its name persisted for a while in the name of an electrical goods shop opened nearby, 'Gem Discount' (714, Burnley Road).

[5] Site of Gem Theatre, Cornholme, 2016, Kate Higham

B.O.S. Cinema Hall, Cornholme
(Closed)

Screening films in 1917, but difficult to trace exactly when it was closed down, although it is still listed as a going concern in 'Barrett's Directory of Blackburn and Burnley 1930-1931'.

Hippodrome Theatre, Halifax Road, Todmorden

The Hippodrome opened as a live theatre on 9th October 1908. It had seating for 1,500 people in stalls and balcony. By 1911, film interludes were part of the dramatic programme and 1917 saw films as the main entertainment.

The external facade is a plain red brick affair, but the auditorium is decorated with Edwardian Baroque style plasterwork. The auditorium remains very much as it was built except for the rear of the stalls, beneath the balcony, which has been walled off to provide a large foyer. It now seats 495 people.

The cinema closed in 1956 and was then taken on by the Todmorden Players and the Todmorden Operatic Society, who still own it. Much renovation has been carried out over the years and it is now a popular venue for theatrical productions and film shows.

[6] Hippodrome Theatre, Todmorden 2016, Kate Higham

136

New Olympia Cinema, Burnley Road, Todmorden (Demolished)

The Olympia Cinema, a corrugated iron structure, was built on this site in 1908, and opened as a skating rink in 1909. It began to show films in 1910, but then closed and was demolished in May 1931 to make way for the New Olympia Cinema.

The Art Deco New Olympia Cinema was opened by the Mayor of Todmorden on 25th August 1932. It had a seating capacity of 1,500, a full stage, and soon became one of the most popular places of entertainment in the town.

In 1955 it was taken over by the Star Cinemas chain, but it eventually closed as a cinema in 1966, when it became the 'Star Bingo Club'.

When the bingo club closed, the elegant Art Deco interior was ripped out to make way for conversion into a supermarket which survived until 2007. The building then sadly stood unused and derelict, until it was finally demolished in May 2016.

[7] New Olympia Cinema, Todmorden, Roger Birch Collection

[8] New Olympia Cinema prior to demolition, 2016, Paul Knights

[9] New Olympia Cinema demolition, 2016, Paul Knights

Palace Cinema, Sowerby Bridge
(Closed)

This cinema was situated on Town Hall Street and was managed by the Greene Brothers in 1917.

The Roxy Cinema, Wharf Street, Sowerby Bridge
(Closed)

Situated alongside the canal in Sowerby Bridge, this cinema was not as grand as some other picture palaces of the day. Originally called The Electric Theatre, it opened in November 1915. It had seating for 812 people in stalls and one tier of balcony.

From 1928 it was owned by Gaumont British Theatres, and then in May 1952 it was taken over by Star Cinemas, when it was re-named Roxy Cinema. It closed in February 1963 and remained empty and unused for nine years before it was re-opened as a bingo club in 1972. Bingo was played in the former balcony, while there was dining in the stalls area.

In 2010 it was converted into a night club and bar called The Roxy Venue.

[10] Roxy Cinema, Sowerby Bridge, 2008, Copyright Betty Longbottom and licensed for reuse under this Creative Commons Licence - https://creativecommons.org/licenses/by-sa/2.0/

[11] Roxy Cinema, 2016, Kate Higham

Essoldo Cinema, Sowerby Bridge
(Demolished, but facade preserved)

This picture house originally opened as the Regent Cinema in 1939. It was taken over by Essoldo Cinemas in 1949, a Mr. Solomon Sheckman's company. Incidentally, the company is named after his family names - ESther (his wife), SOLomon and DOrothy (his daughter).

Closed in 1967, the building was subsequently used as a Regal Bingo hall. When this closed, it lay empty for some years, before being opened as a nightclub in 1972.

The building was demolished in 1987, although the facade was retained as the frontage to retail premises, known as Regent Parade.

[12] Frontage of Essoldo Cinema, Sowerby Bridge, 2016, Kate Higham

Cosy Cinema, Bolton Brow, Sowerby Bridge (Demolished)

Situated on Bolton Brow in Sowerby Bridge, this cinema was recorded as operational in 1917, when it was managed by the Greene Brothers, who also owned several others in the local area.

Originally opened as a chapel, the building was also used to serve dinner to children from the local school.

[13] Site of Cosy Cinema, 2016, (cinema was on opposite side of road just before junction), Kate Higham

Pioneer Cinema, Lee Mount, Halifax (Destroyed by fire)

The Pioneer Cinema was situated in Lee Mount, Halifax. It was nicknamed 'The Knocker' and had capacity for 633 people. It was later renamed The Ritz Cinema, but closed when it was destroyed by fire in 1963.

Picturedrome Cinema, 47 Queens Road, Halifax (Closed)

The Picturedrome Cinema opened in 1912, with the capacity to seat 540 people. It was subsequently renamed The Kingston Picture House, and then The Lyric Cinema, but closed its doors on 13th July, 1951. It has since been used to house a bathroom showroom.

[14] Picturedrome Cinema 2016, Kate Higham

Cosy Cinema, 238 Queens Road, Halifax (Closed)

The Cosy Cinema, situated on Queens Road in Halifax, has also been known as The Cosy Corner Picture Palace. It opened in 1914 and was able to seat 698 people. By 1953, it had been taken over by the Star Cinemas chain but, unfortunately, it closed as a cinema in 1964 and was converted into retail premises.

[15] *Cosy Cinema, Halifax, Halifax Courier*

[16] *Cosy Cinema, 2016, Kate Higham*

144

Palladium Cinema, 163 King Cross Road, Halifax (Closed)

The Palladium Cinema was opened in 1914 by a private company, Palladium Pictures Limited. It had seating for 895 people in stalls and a small balcony. This rather unusual balcony only projected about three quarters of the way across the stalls and had only seven rows of seats.

Star Cinemas took the cinema over in 1944, and renamed it The New Palladium Cinema. It closed in 1962 to make way for a bingo hall, but is now retail premises.

If one ventures inside, some of the the interior is still intact. The balcony is still in place, complete with gilt lion's head.

[17] Palladium Cinema, Halifax, 2016, Kate Higham

[18] Interior of Palladium Cinema showing balcony, 2016, Kate Higham

[19] Palladium Cinema interior, lion's head detail still in place, 2016, Kate Higham

146

The Alhambra, St. James Road, Halifax
(Demolished)

The Oddfellows' Hall opened its doors on 6th June 1840. It was a magnificent building with four Corinthian columns supporting a pediment. Its architect was Charles Child, who also designed several churches in the area during his career.

It was used for concerts and theatrical performances. Franz Liszt performed there on 29th January 1841, and Charles Dickens visited on 16th September 1858 to give a two hour reading from 'A Christmas Carol'. Dickens was not particularly taken with Halifax as, after his visit, he was quoted as saying:

"Halifax was too small for us. I never saw such an audience though. They were really worth reading to for nothing, though I didn't exactly do that. It is as horrible a place as I ever saw, I think".(11)

The building also housed the Royal Hotel, which had stables, and rooms for travelling members of the Oddfellows organisation.

The auditorium was converted into a music hall in 1888 and, in 1900, it was renamed The People's Palace.

Films were first screened there in 1917 and, in 1920, it was renamed The Alhambra Picture House, but later became known as The Alhambra Cinema, with seating for 737 people.

The building was purchased by Halifax Council in 1955, at which point it housed the cinema and a small dance school. The cinema continued to operate until it closed on 20th June 1959.

The building was demolished in August 1963 and the site is now a car park.

[20] Alhambra Cinema, Halifax, Copyright Ken Roe and licensed for reuse under this Creative Commons (Attribution) License http://cinematreasures.org/theaters/39767/photos/113020

[21] Site of Alhambra Cinema, 2016, Kate Higham

Ideal Pictures, Halifax
(Demolished)

Little detail seems to remain regarding this cinema. It was operational on Raglan Street, Halifax, but closed in 1917.

The Odeon Cinema, Broad Street, Halifax
(Closed)

The Odeon Cinema opened in June 1938 with seating for 2,058 in stalls and balcony. It was designed by prominent cinema architect of the day, George Coles, and cost £59,727 to build. The facade was decorated with light coloured tiles and its tall art deco tower was lit up with an 'ODEON' sign. It reportedly had a lavish interior, the auditorium dominated by bas-relief female figures mounted either side of the screen.

The Odeon also served as a live venue for concerts and other functions. During the Second World War, many events were held here to raise funds for the war effort. Between 1959 and 1964, it played host to many popular music concerts. Cliff Richard & the Shadows, Billy Fury, Gene Vincent and Dusty Springfield all played here during this period.

The cinema closed in 1975 and remained unused for some time before being converted to a bingo hall.

[22] *Odeon Cinema, Halifax, Copyright odeon and licensed for reuse under this Creative Commons (Attribution) License - http://cinematreasures.org/theaters/3330/ photos/6424*

[23] *Odeon Cinema, 2016, Kate Higham*

Gem Cinema, Crossley Street, Halifax
(Closed)

This building started life as The Mechanics' Institute in 1857. It then became known as Marlborough Hall and was used as a concert hall, seating 700. Films were shown here from about 1896, making it the first cinema in Halifax. It became known as The Gem, and then, in 1917, it was officially opened as The Gem Cinema by the Greene Brothers (who owned a chain of cinemas).

It closed its doors in 1932 and became a dance academy, but then it was taken over by the YMCA in 1946. This organisation still use the building for events, shows and roller-skating.

[24] The Gem Cinema, Halifax, 2016, Kate Higham

Cinema de Luxe, Halifax
(Demolished)

Northgate House, which once stood adjacent to the site of this cinema, was once the home of Joseph and Mary Lister. Joseph Lister was uncle to Anne Lister, well-known local land-owner, traveller and chronicler. When Anne inherited the house, she converted it into a hotel, Northgate Hotel.

Next to the hotel she built Northgate Hall to function as an assembly hall and meeting place. The foundation stone for this building was laid by Anne Lister and Ann Walker in 1835. They buried a time capsule under the stone containing coins and an engraved lead scroll.

In 1860, Northgate Hall was leased by the Temperance Society and used as a Temperance Hall. In 1912, it was converted into a cinema, known as the Cinema de Luxe, which could seat 550 people.

The cinema's name was changed to the Theatre de Luxe in 1914 and, incidentally, the infamous serial killer, John Christie, worked as a projectionist here in around 1920.

In 1934, the cinema's name was changed yet again, this time to the Roxy de Luxe. It remained operational for only a few more years after this, however, and closed in 1938.

The hotel and cinema were demolished in 1959. At this point, the time capsule was found and given to Calderdale Museums for safe-keeping.

[25] Theatre de Luxe, Northgate Halifax, Steve Gee Collection

[26] Site of Theatre de Luxe, Northgate, Halifax, 2016, Kate Higham

153

The Grand Cinema, North Bridge, Halifax
(Demolished)

The Grand Cinema was built on the site of the old, wooden-built Gaiety Theatre. It was originally called The Grand Theatre and Opera House, was designed by renowned theatre architect, Frank Matcham, and opened on 5th August 1889. Seating for 1,650 people was provided in stalls, dress circle, and upper circle, and there were two stage boxes and six private boxes. ERA magazine at the time reported:

"Crimson velvet has been used in the upholstering of the boxes, stalls, and circles; the corridors are laid with Brussels carpets; and the walls of the circles are papered in crimson and gold. The internal decorations have all been carried out by Messrs Jonas Binns and Sons, of Halifax, the prevailing colour being electric blue on a cream ground relieved with gold. Behind the curtain the comfort of the artists has been well looked after, the dressing-rooms being fitted with every convenience. On the stage the latest appliances are in use, and an iron curtain shuts off the stage from the auditorium."(12)

In 1896, it was taken over by Northern Theatre Companies Limited and, from 1903, became a variety theatre. Films were shown as part of the live programme from 1911 and, in 1925, it was converted into a full-time cinema known as the Grand Picture House. It had a rear projection box built on the stage. It was renamed the Grand Cinema in the early 1940's.

Around 1954 it closed as a cinema and was taken over briefly by the Halifax Theatre Repertory Co. when it became the Grand Theatre. This closed in May 1956 when there was a major fall of ornamental plasterwork from the ceiling in the auditorium. The building never re-opened and was demolished in 1958. The site is currently used as a car park, although the rear wall remains in place.

[27] Grand Cinema, Halifax, (cinema on right at front of picture), Copyright Mike Blakemore, and licensed for reuse under this Creative Commons (Attribution) License, http://cinematreasures.org/theaters/38774/photos/62845,

[28] Site of Grand Cinema, 2016, Kate Higham

Theatre Royal, Southgate, Halifax
(Closed)

The original theatre on this site was built in 1789. This was demolished, however, to make way for the current building which opened in August 1905 as a live entertainment venue. Its superb facade, in the Edwardian style, is built of ashlar stone. There was once a cast iron canopy over the entrance to protect those alighting from carriages to visit the theatre. The auditorium of the theatre had four tiers.

In 1927, a massive fire swept through the building, destroying the stage and backstage area. The auditorium was saved due to the fire curtain installed at the front of the stage and, after a rebuild, the theatre was able to re-open later that same year.

In 1933, the building was converted for use as a cinema, with just two tiers in the auditorium, and seating for 1,549 people. The Theatre Royal Cinema operated until 1966, when it was closed and converted into a bingo hall. This closed in 1992 and it has, over time, been reincarnated as a nightclub, a Chinese restaurant, and a bar. By 2007, these had closed and the building was empty and unused. The facade is Grade II Listed.

[29] Theatre Royal, Halifax, Copyright Mike Blakemore and licensed for reuse under this Creative Commons (Attribution) License - http://cinematreasures.org/theaters/3329/photos/53788

[30] Theatre Royal, 2016, Kate Higham

National Cinema, Halifax
(Closed)

Screening films in 1917, the National Cinema was on Commercial Street, Halifax.

ABC Cinema, Wards End, Halifax
(Closed)

This was built as The Regal and opened in September 1938. It was described as an extremely fine cinema with 1,250 seats in the stalls area and 688 in the balcony. The proscenium was surrounded by elaborate plaster fretwork panels hiding ventilation ducts. In niches on each side stood tall, slender figures rather like Oscar statuettes.

It was renamed The ABC Cinema in 1961 and, after alterations in 1976, it re-opened with three screens. At this point, it was renamed The Cannon Cinema, but soon afterwards reverted to The ABC.

In 2000, it obtained a Grade II listing which ensured that most of the elements of the original building were preserved. The cinema closed in 2002 and was converted into a nightclub.

[31] ABC Cinema, Halifax, Copyright Terry and licensed for reuse under this Creative Commons (Attribution) License - http://cinematreasures.org/theaters/3331/photos/132646

[32] ABC Cinema, 2016, Kate Higham

Picture House Cinema, Wards End, Halifax (Closed)

The Picture House opened here in 1913. It was built by Provincial Cinematograph Theatres and was then passed on to Gaumont British Theatres. In 1947, it was closed after a serious fire and, when it re-opened, it was named The Gaumont. It closed in 1960 and remained unused for several years before re-opening as a Top Rank Bingo Club. This was sold to Hutchinson Leisure in 1973 and became a Surewin Bingo Club.

Later, the balcony was converted into two small cinemas, Astra 1 & 2, whilst bingo continued on the lower floor. These screens closed in 1982 and, a few years later, the building was transformed into a nightclub called the Coliseum. Since 2011, it has operated as Liquid Nightclub.

THE PICTURE HOUSE, HALIFAX. Lilywhite Series.

[33] Picture House Cinema, Halifax, Copyright Mike Blakemore and licensed for reuse under this Creative Commons (Attribution) License - http://cinematreasures.org/ theaters/3332/photos/45132

The Electric Theatre, 70-72 Commercial Street, Halifax (Closed)

The building dates back to the late nineteenth century when it housed a riding school. The conversion from riding school into a cinema, known as The Electric Theatre, took place in 1911.

The cinema had 800 seats and was part of the National Electric Circuit. Taken over in 1928 by Gaumont, it was enlarged to accommodate 1,100 people. A few years later, it was enlarged again and was then able to seat 1,728 people.

The building was given a new facade and modernised in 1939, when its capacity was reduced to 1,536.

In 1956, it closed as a cinema and at various times served as a car show room, a DIY store, and then a snooker club.

In 2005, it was renovated with yet another facade and converted to house a bowling alley and a bar on the ground floor, and a snooker club on the first floor. It was named 'The Electric Bowl' at this time.

[34] Electric Theatre, Halifax, Copyright Mike Blakemore and licensed for reuse under this Creative Commons (Attribution) License, http://cinematreasures.org/theaters/21875/photos/78502

[35] Electric Theatre, 2016 (now called 'Electric Bowl'), Kate Higham

Rex Cinema, Coronation Street, Elland

This is one of the oldest structurally unaltered cinemas in the country. Opened as the Central Picture House in 1912, it closed in 1959, but re-opened later the same year as the Rex. It has had several other closures and re-openings during its life-time.

It ceased operating during the general recession in the cinema industry in 1964, and was then converted to a bingo hall. It was shut down in 1985 in a dilapidated state. It would have remained derelict but for the intervention of businessmen, Charles Morris and Peter Berry, who purchased it and had it refurbished.

It re-opened in October 1988 and has since prospered under their guidance. There is a resident organist who plays the 'Conn 651' theatre organ during the intervals between films. Also very popular are the regularly staged concerts.

The screen is at the front of the building, which is rare.

[36] Rex Cinema, Elland, 2016, Kate Higham

Palladium Cinema, Southgate, Elland
(Closed)

Elland Town Hall was opened in 1888. It began screening films in 1909, and became known as The Palladium Cinema. The cinema closed in 1959.

[37] Elland Town Hall, Palladium Cinema, 2016, Kate Higham

Albert Theatre & Opera House, Brighouse (Closed)

The Albert Hall opened in 1899, accommodating 1,100 people in three tiers of seating. Around 1908, it was renamed The New Albert Theatre and was regularly showing short films alongside live variety entertainment.

In 1929, the interior was rebuilt to have just one tier of balcony.

In 1953, it was taken over by Star Cinemas, who installed CinemaScope. During the 1960's, on a couple of nights each week, it converted to a Star Bingo Hall (a part of the Star group of companies).

It closed as a cinema in 1972 and became a bingo hall and social club. Recently, it has been converted into a bar/restaurant called 'The Calder'.

[38] Albert Theatre 2016, Brighouse, Kate Higham

Empire Theatre, Brighouse
(Demolished)

The Atlas Mill Roller-Skating Rink was built on the site of Atlas Mill in Brighouse in 1909. In 1911, it was converted into a cinema, the rink, however, being retained so that cinema-goers could skate in the intermission! In 1917, it was re-named The Empire Theatre. It shut after about a year and the building was demolished during World War I.
The site now houses a mobile home development.

[39] The site of The Empire Theatre, Brighouse, 2016, Copyright Humphrey Bolton and licensed for re-use under this Creative Commons (Attribution) license - http://www.geograph.org.uk/photo/1177054

Savoy Cinema, Brighouse
(Closed)

Films were shown in Brighouse Civic Hall around 1900, when it became known as The Savoy Cinema. Screenings ceased in 1959.

[40] Brighouse Civic Hall, Savoy Cinema, 2016, Kate Higham

Ritz Cinema, 73 Bradford Road, Brighouse
(Closed)

The Ritz, Brighouse, opened its doors in 1937 and operated as a cinema continuously until 1961. It was run by the ABC Cinema Group for most of this time.

It was used as a bingo hall for a very short period of time, but was then converted into The New Ritz Ballroom. It is now named Live at the Ritz and operates as a live event venue.

[41] Ritz Cinema, 2016, Kate Higham

APPENDIX 2

Filming In and Around Hebden Bridge

Helen of Four Gates (1920)

'Helen of Four Gates', directed by Cecil Hepworth, is adapted from the novel of the same name, written by Ethel Carnie Holdsworth. A melodrama, set and filmed on the moors around Heptonstall and Hebden Bridge, the film stars Alma Taylor as Helen (both mother and daughter), James Carew, George Dewhurst and John MacAndrews.

Helen was entrusted to the care of her mother's ex-suitor when both of her parents died. The ex-suitor, Abel, determines to extract revenge on her mother for rejecting him by making Helen's life as miserable as possible.

It is a dramatic, gritty tale of retribution and thwarted love, with a message to tell of how men held the reins of power in society at that time.

Born in 1886, Ethel Carnie Holdsworth grew up in Lancashire and worked in the mills from an early age. She was politically active, campaigning against conscription in World War I, a feminist, and was one of the first published working class female writers in the UK. Her first publications were poetry collections - 'Rhymes from the Factory' (1907), 'Songs of a Factory Girl' (1911) and 'Voices of Womanhood' (1914). Ethel produced several successful novels and she also regularly wrote for feminist and socialist magazines.

She moved to Hebden Bridge with her husband and daughters in the 1920's. Her early experiences of hard labour and grim conditions in the mills clearly inspired her work.

In 'Our Right to Play' she writes:
"For God's sake, women, go out and play.
Instead of staring round to see what wants polishing or rubbing, go out into the open and draw the breath of the moors or the hills into your lungs. Get some of the starshine and sunlight into your souls, and do not forget that you are something more than a dish washer - that you are more necessary to the human race than politicians - or anything."(13)

[1] Helen of Four Gates, Copyright Hepworth, 1920

[2] Helen of Four Gates, Copyright Hepworth, 1920

A Boy, A Girl and A Bike (1949)

'A Boy, A Girl and A Bike' is directed by Ralph Smart from a script co-written by Ted Willis.

Ted Willis was credited in the Guiness Book of World Records as the world's most prolific television script-writer! Noted for television's 'Dixon of Dock Green', he also successfully wrote many stage plays, novels and feature films, and was awarded a life-time peerage in 1963.

Before World War II, director Ralph Smart was involved in making 'quota quickies' - low-budget films made to satisfy legal requirements regarding the proportion of British-made films shown in U.K. cinemas. After the War, however, he was employed by Rank Organisation, and it was from there that he directed 'A Boy, A Girl and A Bike'.

The stars of this film are Honor Blackman, John Mc Callum, Patrick Holt and Diana Dors although other household names, such as Thora Hird and Anthony Newley, also appear.

In this light-hearted romantic film, set in a fictitious Yorkshire mill town, Wakeford, the main characters are members of the local cycling club, The Wakeford Wheelers. There is romance with a love triangle, road races, cycle theft, illegal gambling, dancing and a deserting soldier among the action. Produced during the heyday of British cinema, 'A Boy, A Girl and A Bike' would have been relevant to young people of the day, as cycling, dancing and cinema were all popular organised pastimes.

The stunning location photography in this film is worthy of mention in itself. The film is shot in Calderdale, around Hebden Bridge, Halifax and Mytholmroyd, and also in North Yorkshire, in areas including Skipton, Burnsall, Yockenthwaite, Grassington and Malham.

[3] 'A Boy, A Girl and A Bike', Honor Blackman on Bridge Lanes, Hebden Bridge, Copyright Gainsborough Pictures, 1949

[4] 'A Boy, A Girl and A Bike', Riders on Boothtown Road, heading into Halifax, Copyright Gainsborough Pictures, 1949

173

Fanny and Elvis (1999)

'Fanny and Elvis' is written and directed by Kay Mellor. A romantic comedy, set at the turn of the millenium, it was almost entirely filmed in Hebden Bridge. Many local people appeared as extras and St George's Square was covered in fake snow for some scenes.

The plot concerns Kate, a writer, who discovers that her biological clock is ticking just as her husband announces that he is leaving her. She takes in Dave, a brash Cockney car salesman, as a lodger. It emerges that Dave's former partner is the woman for whom Kate's husband has left her. The film follows Kate and Dave as their relationship develops. The writing is warm and witty, a definite 'feel good' film.

The cast include Kerry Fox, Ray Winstone, Ben Daniels, David Morrisey, Jennifer Saunders, Colin Salmon, Gaynor Faye (Kay Mellor's daughter) and Michael Medwin. Ray Winstone, particularly, received good reviews for his portrayal of Dave - a break-away from his usual 'tough guy' image!

Kay Mellor is a writer, director and actress, who was born and still lives in Leeds. She worked as a script-writer for 'Coronation Street' in the '80's, before moving on to write many highly acclaimed TV dramas. These include 'Band of Gold', 'Playing the Field', 'Fat Friends', 'Strictly Confidential', 'The Chase', 'The Syndicate' and 'In the Club'. She has appeared in her own adaptation of 'Jane Eyre', and other dramas such as 'Stan the Man' and 'Gifted'. Kay Mellor was awarded an O.B.E. in the 2009 Birthday Honours List.

[5] Kerry Fox and Ray Winstone, 'Fanny and Elvis', Copyright United International
Pictures, 1999

[6] Jennifer Saunders and Kerry Fox, 'Fanny and Elvis' Copyright United International
Pictures, 1999

175

The Tyre (2000)

'The Tyre' was made with the support of The Film Council, Film Four, the Yorkshire Media Production Agency and Yorkshire Arts. It is a film adaptation of the poem 'The Tyre' by Simon Armitage.

The film depicts a sales rep, played by Christopher Eccleston, who feels trapped and frustrated by his life and job. One day a business trip takes him back to the town where he grew up, and when his car develops a flat tyre, he has to stop to change it. As the spare tyre runs down a hill away from him he is transported back to his childhood, when he and some friends found a tractor tyre and sent it rolling downhill out of control.

'The Tyre' screenplay was written by Simon Armitage and Brian Hill, and directed by Brian Hill. The music was composed by Julian Stewart Lindsay.

The film won the Yorkshire Film Award at the Leeds International Film Festival 2001. The comment from the judges:

"The Tyre was selected for its stunning use of landscape and locations, superb cinematography and wonderful script. It's a beautifully realised film that appeals to all ages."

Interestingly, Christopher Eccleston also appeared in 'Killing Time', a feature length film of Simon Armitage's 1,000 line millennium poem of the same name, which was also directed by Brian Hill. It was shown on television on New Year's Day 2000.

[7] (left) Simon Armitage, Copyright Alexander Williamson and licensed for re-use under this Creative Commons license - https://creativecommons.org/ licenses/by/2.0/deed.en

[8] (right) Christopher Eccleston, Copyright jamin2 and licensed for re-use under this Creative Commons license - https://creativecommons.org/ licenses/by/2.0/deed.en

177

Nicholas Nickleby (2002)

'Nicholas Nickleby' is a drama film based on the novel 'The Life and Adventures of Nicholas Nickleby' by Charles Dickens. This book was originally published weekly in serial form between 1838 and 1839.

The story follows the fortunes of a young man, Nicholas Nickleby (Charlie Hunnam), whose father dies, leaving him to look after his mother (Stella Gonet) and sister, Kate (Romola Garai). Nicholas contacts his Uncle Ralph (Christopher Plummer) who secures a job for him at Dotheboy's Hall, a grim, cruelly-run school supervised by Wackford Squeers (Jim Broadbent) and Mrs Squeers (Juliet Stevenson). Whilst he is at the school, his uncle turns his mother and sister out of their home, and uses his sister as bait, to entice other merchants to do business with him. Nicholas escapes from Dotheboys Hall with Smike (Jamie Bell), a former pupil at the school, and then sets about trying to save the rest of his family.

The screenplay was written and directed by Douglas McGrath. Apart from the actors named above, the cast also included Tom Courtenay, Alan Cumming, Edward Fox, Anne Hathaway, Barry Humphries, Nathan Lane and Timothy Spall.

The film received good reviews following its release. It won the 2002 National Board of Review (USA) Award for Best Acting by an Ensemble, and was nominated for the 2003 Golden Globe Award for Best Motion Picture - Musical or Comedy.

Gibson Mill at Hardcastle Crags, Hebden Bridge, was used as the location for Dotheboys Hall. The mill building, opened around 1800 as a cotton mill, provided a suitably atmospheric, brooding backdrop to the story.

[9] Above, Gibson Mill, Hebden Bridge, Kate Higham

[10] Below, 'Nicholas Nickleby', 2002, Copyright United Artists

My Summer of Love (2004)

'My Summer of Love' is a film based on the novel of the same name by Helen Cross. Directed by Pawel Pawlikowski, the screenplay was co-written by Pawel Pawlikowski and Michael Wynne.

The film explores themes of obsession and deception. Mona (Natalie Press) lives with her brother, Phil (Paddy Considine) above a pub. Her brother converted to Christianity whilst in prison. Mona meets Tamsin (Emily Blunt), who is privileged and spoilt, and the two girls find themselves fascinated by each other. Their relationship quickly becomes intense and sexual as they each vow to kill the other if they are betrayed.

Upon release, 'My Summer of Love' received excellent reviews. It went on to win the 2005 BAFTA for Best British Film, the 2005 Directors Guild of Great Britain Award for Outstanding Directorial Achievement in British Film, the 2004 Edinburgh International Film Festival Award for Best New British Feature, the 2005 Evening Standard British Film Award for Best Screenplay and Most Promising Newcomer (Blunt and Press) and the 2005 London Critics Circle Film Award.

Many of the outdoor scenes were filmed in Cornholme and the film location used for the pub where Mona lived was The Swan in Bacup. The ballroom scene was filmed at the Live at the Ritz venue in Brighouse which, you may remember, was once The Ritz cinema.

[11] 'My Summer of Love' on location, Cornholme, Copyright Apocalypso Pictures, 2004

[12] 'My Summer of Love', Natalie Press & Emily Blunt, Copyright Apocalypso Pictures, 2004

181

Shed Your Tears and Walk Away (2009)

A documentary film made by Jez Lewis and produced by his company, Bungalow Town Productions, this film explores the problems of alcoholism, substance abuse and suicide in Hebden Bridge. Because so many of his personal friends had been affected by these problems, Jez Lewis returned to his hometown, Hebden Bridge, with a personal quest: to try to understand why such a supposedly idyllic town seemed to have such a dark, troubled side.

Jez followed the fortunes of several Hebden Bridge residents, all fighting their own battles with alcohol, substance abuse or mental illness. The film is truly made from the heart and Jez was quoted as saying of the experience, *"I know that I have made a difference to some individuals, particularly those I have been connected with in the film."*

At the time of release, the film caused much discussion and debate in Hebden Bridge. Some believed that the town was particularly troubled by these problems for reasons such as unemployment, housing issues secondary to 'gentrification', its possible position on a drug-trafficking route, or even weather conditions. Cllr Nader Fekri felt that it was important to realise that, although the film concentrated on the problems of alcohol, drug abuse and suicide in Hebden Bridge, these issues were equally worrying in all communities. He said of the film, *"While it focused on Hebden Bridge, there is a bigger picture about drugs within our society in communities big and small."*

Having won the Best U.K. First Feature Award at the East End Film Festival 2010, it was also nominated for Best Documentary on a Contemporary Theme at the Grierson Awards 2011.

Mark Kermode, reviewing the film for The Observer, said, *"Jez Lewis's documentary is something special – a poetic, powerful and often very painful film made with a raw intimacy that bespeaks harsh truths."*

[13] Jez Lewis with Michael Silcock, filming for 'Shed Your Tears and Walk Away', 2009, photograph courtesy of Jez Lewis

[14] Jez Lewis filming 'Shed Your Tears and Walk Away' in Calder Holmes Park, Hebden Bridge, 2009, Photograph courtesy of Jez Lewis

The Rochdale Pioneers (2012)

'The Rochdale Pioneers' was commissioned and funded by the Cooperative Group to be part of the United Nations International Year of Cooperatives, 2012. Produced by the Cooperative British Youth Film Academy, it was directed by John Montegrande and Adam Lee Hamilton from a screenplay written by J.S. Papenbrock. Local Rochdale residents were recruited to appear in the film, alongside established actors such as John Henshaw and John McArdle.

The film is set in the 1840's, when a group of Rochdale men, disillusioned by local shops and traders selling poor quality goods at extortionate prices, formed the Rochdale Equitable Pioneers Society. They opened a small shop, determined to sell their stock at fair prices, sharing the profits with their customers. Their success grew, and other fledgling cooperatives around the country began to adopt their ideas and methods. Eventually, their revolutionary approach to business gained the international reputation which lives on today.

A documentary, 'The Making of 'The Rochdale Pioneers'', was released to accompany the film. This was directed and produced by Darren White.

'The Rochdale Pioneers' was premiered in Manchester in November 2012 as part of the United Nations International Year of Cooperatives.

Some scenes were shot at Rochdale Town Hall and The Rochdale Pioneers Museum, but the location used to film village scenes for 'The Rochdale Pioneers' was Heptonstall.

[15] *John Henshaw, Andrew London and Jordan Dawes (left to right), 'The Rochdale Pioneers', Copyright British Youth Film Academy, 2012*

[16] *'The Rochdale Pioneers', Copyright British Youth Film Academy, 2012*

Swallows and Amazons (2016)

This adaptation of Arthur Ransome's 'Swallows and Amazons' was written by Andrea Gibb and directed by Philippa Lowthorpe. The cast included Andrew Scott, Rafe Spall, Kelly Macdonald, Jessica Hynes, and Harry Enfield.

The film, updated to 1935 from the original 1929 setting, depicts the adventures of four children on holiday in the Lake District. They sail their boat, 'The Swallow' to an island in the middle of a lake, but find that a rival group of children, with their boat, 'The Amazon', have already laid claim to it. The struggle commences as the children vie for supremacy on the island.

Whilst the novel focuses on these battles, along with the children's dealings with the Amazons' uncle who lives on a house-boat nearby, the adaptation introduces more dramatic themes, such as espionage, into the plot.

Locations used in the Lake District included Coniston Water and Derwent Water, and the film was premiered at The Theatre by The Lake in Keswick in August 2016.

Other locations used included Plumpton Rocks, Keighley Worth Valley Railway and Heptonstall.

[17] & [18] (above & below) Filming for 'Swallows and Amazons' in Heptonstall, Pictures courtesy of Bruce Cutts, After Alice Project

Stet Fortuna Domus